FEAR MACS NO MORE

Danny Goodman

D1158735

Fear Macs No More

Danny Goodman

New York   London   Toronto   Sydney   Tokyo   Singapore

Copyright © 1993 by Danny Goodman

All rights reserved, including the right of reproduction in whole or in part in any form.

Brady Publishing

A Division of Prentice Hall Computer Publishing
15 Columbus Circle
New York, NY 10023

ISBN: 1-56686-082-2
Library of Congress Catalog No.: 93-9562

Printing Code: The rightmost double-digit number is the year of the book's printing; the rightmost single-digit number is the number of the book's printing. For example, 93-1 shows that the first printing of the book occurred in 1993.

96   95   94   93   4   3   2   1

Manufactured in the United States of America

Limits of Liability and Disclaimer of Warranty: The author and publisher of this book have used their best efforts in preparing this book and the programs contained in it. These efforts include the development, research, and testing of the theories and programs to determine their effectiveness. The author and publisher make no warranty of any kind, expressed or implied, with regard to these programs or the documentation contained in this book. The author and publisher shall not be liable in any event for incidental or consequential damages in connection with, or arising out of, the furnishing, performance, or use of these programs.

Trademarks: Most computer and software brand names have trademarks or registered trademarks. The individual trademarks have not been listed here.

About the Author

Danny Goodman has been translating high-tech information for non-technical readers since the mid 1970s. He is a frequent contributor to *Playboy*, in-flight magazines, and city magazines across the country. His personal computer writing history spans the time of early *PC Magazine* to *PC World*, *MacWorld*, and *MacUser*. Author of 14 books on personal computers, his *Complete HyperCard Handbook* was a bestseller. With world-class information designer, Richard Saul Wurman, the *Danny Goodman's Macintosh Handbook* broke new ground in computer book organization and presentation. Danny lives in a small coastal community near San Francisco.

Acknowledgment

A number of people deserve recognition for their help in turning an idea into reality. Because their roles are equally important within their specialities, I thank these folks in alphabetical order: Kelly Dobbs, Bill Gladstone, Jono Hardjowirogo, Deborah Robbins, Steve Ruddock, Nathan Shedroff, Martha Steffen, and Mike Violano. Perhaps, the biggest thanks goes to the thousands of people I've met over the years who rolled their eyes when they heard I worked with computers and then rattled on about how they need to figure out how to use a machine one of these days. Today is the day.

Credits

Publisher
Michael Violano

Acquisitions Director
Jono Hardjowirogo

Managing Editor
Kelly D. Dobbs

Editorial Assistant
Lisa Rose

Illustrator
John Leonard Gieg

Book Designer
Michele Laseau

Cover Designer
Jay Corpus

Production Team
Diana Bigham, Katy Bodenmiller, Jeanne Clark, Scott Cook,
Tim Cox, Mark Enochs, Linda Koopman, Tom Loveman,
Roger S. Morgan, Joe Ramon, Carrie Roth, Greg Simsic, Craig Small

Contents

Introduction

Why You're Afraid
(and What We're Going To Do About It)

Here is a scene familiar to many...Your airliner has just arrived in a city you've never visited before. You walk through the jetway into the strange airport terminal gate area. You have a job to do: visiting clients, some of whom you already know from telephone conversations; others are complete strangers. Appointments were set before you left home, and you obviously want to be prompt (even if one of the big shots you're seeing should keep you waiting in the lobby for an hour).

First, you have to find the rental car desk. Because you're not really sure where they are at this airport, you follow the signs to baggage claim and ground transportation.

"Do you want a subcompact, compact, midsize, standard, or luxury car?" the rental agent asks. You have a vague notion of what a luxury model might be (and the consequences of listing one on your expense report), but the others are up for grabs. "A midsize," you say after some hesitation, but with a forcefulness that implies you were really thinking about the differences among the models you would get at each size. After a few clicks on the agent's computer terminal comes the offer, "We can give you a Celestial, a 3000K, or a Palomino convertible." You've seen glimpses of TV ads for some of these as you flipped channels, but you don't have a clue which is the best car. "I'll take the Celestial," you say, shrugging your shoulders. A couple of minutes and a few "initial heres" later, the agent whips out the following verbal instructions for the umpteenth time today, "Take the escalator to the departure level, cross to the outer island, go to the blue zone, and flag down our green and red van. Next in line?" You turn away hoping to look like an old pro, but into your mind flood questions like, "Is that up or down? How much traffic do I have to cross to get to that outer island? How far is it, anyway? What were those colors again?"

Fortunately, you stumble your way to the island and wave down the van. Assuming that you survive the Tilt-a-Whirl ride to the rental lot, you get into a strange car whose dashboard is loaded with more buttons than you've ever seen. You're freezing, and the air conditioner is blowing full force—how do you turn this thing off? How do you find a radio station with the music or talk you like when you can't even figure out how to tune the stations? If it rains later, it will take several minutes to find the wiper control. If you go out to dinner with a client and reach the parking lot in the dark, you'll be fumbling for a headlight switch whose location and feel are not in your fingers. And when you later pull up to refill the gas on your way back, you'll wonder if the gas cap is on the left or right rear fender.

Hand scribbled in your date book are directions to your first stop. You check your watch and see that you're running late if the "it's about 20 minutes from the airport" advice was correct...and the highway isn't clogged. As you motor your way down unfamiliar roads, the only thing you know about where you are is that at the moment you're taking Fernwiler Boulevard until you reach the fourth stoplight. Your heart rate is certainly heading skyward as you can't find the industrial park driveway that "you can't miss." When you do pull in after your u-turn, all visitor parking spaces are taken, and every other spot you see has somebody's name painted on it. So you look for any spot in outer Mongolia.

After the hike in from the parking lot, you're almost hyperventilating when you announce yourself to the receptionist. You haven't met this client before, so you won't even know the face when the person comes through the door, bidding you to enter. How will your first impression be? Is your hair neat? Are your clothing apertures closed? Finally you meet, enter the conference room, and exchange pleasantries. Then you start talking about the subject of your visit. Now you can relax, because you're in familiar territory, and you can do your job.

Fear Is Natural

A traveling executive may be loathe to admit it, but fear plays a big role in responses to things that happen along a trip. These fears arise from three sources:

1. Fear of the unknown, especially when technology is involved ("How do I reach my appointment in time and turn on the wipers now that it's raining?")

2. Mystifying and overabundant terminology ("Quick, do you want a subcompact, compact, standard, or midsize?")

3. Fear of looking foolish by asking questions to which you're convinced everyone else in the world has the answers ("I hope signs tell me which escalator takes me to the departure level and where the—what color was that?—zone is.")

Doing the Job—with a Computer

When it comes to using a new personal computer for the first time, we all go through the same trepidation as the harried business traveler. We have a job to do, and the personal computer is one of the tools we can use to accomplish that job—and do the job better than without the machine, we hope. The same fears apply, however:

1. Fear of the unknown, especially when technology is involved ("I never even figured out what all the knobs and levers did on my old typewriter, and now all these keyboard keys and cables are coming to get me!")

2. Mystifying and overabundant terminology ("I don't understand half the advertisements for the computer I just bought.")

3. Fear of looking foolish by asking questions to which you're convinced everyone else in the world has the answers ("I can't look stupid next to my neighbor's teenager.")

Step One: Relax

To overcome these justifiable fears, it's important to know that there isn't a person alive who knows absolutely everything about the Macintosh and its software library (although you'll find lots of people who *think* they do). Even if you find a very knowledgeable Macintosh guru, you know something far more valuable to you than all the technical wizardry: what you need to do for your job. That's why you have the job you do or have chosen a particular profession.

This distinction is important. To computer gurus, the computers are the end, the goal, the miracle without which the world implodes. To you, however, the computer is just another tool that can help you do the job. Incorporating the tool into your work comfortably means knowing basic skills so that you can focus on your work, without letting the computer get in your way. Ideally, operating the computer should feel as automatic as operating a vehicle to get from point A to point B; your focus is on point B and what you'll be doing when you get there, not on how internal combustion engines or bicycle gears work.

What We'll Do

My goal is to guide you through the unknown territory that is Macintosh, making you work with the computer in the process. You cannot learn how to use anything without actually using it. For example, if you give those written directions to a new client's office to a taxi driver, how many trips will it take before you know how to get there yourself? But if you drive there yourself, by the third time, you probably won't even think about where you need to turn; you just do it.

I recognize that you are not setting out to be a computer expert. It's more important that you become comfortable with enough Macintosh operation to let you get on with your work life. Because you will inevitably run into things that you don't know or understand, I'll be showing you how to solve problems on your own, ask the right questions when necessary, and get answers quickly. If I can show you what to do when you don't know what to do, you will become an intelligent Macintosh user. In other words, you will *Fear Macs No More*.

How I Do It

My methods are simple. I've distilled the essence of using a Macintosh productively into a series of short encounters, each of which builds on experience gained from previous encounters.

The first 15 encounters are mandatory; the remaining are optional in case earlier discussions have peaked your curiosity (or you suspect you may be having fun). In each encounter, I introduce essential Macintosh terminology and basic principles. If you've come to the Macintosh after exposure to an IBM-compatible (DOS) personal computer, I have sections to help you readily see the differences between those kinds of systems and the Macintosh. I also include sections for you to practice the principles on your Mac so that you can get to feel the rhythms of working with the Mac on your way to making things automatic. I even include some final questions to reinforce the subject, intended to expel your Macintosh fears—I call them exorcises.

Near the end of the book, I go into a section titled "On Your Own." Having reached that stage, you'll be ready to start putting the Macintosh to work in your own environment (a recording of the theme song to *Born Free* would be suitable background music while reading this section).

> **Performa owners note:** Your Macintosh Performa model comes with some extra software (notably *At Ease* and *Launcher*) that simplifies day-to-day operation. Your goal, however, is to learn skills common to *all* Macintosh models, and thus make it easier for you to maximize the Performa's special features later on.

Assumptions

Before you begin, be aware of the only assumption I make about you and your Macintosh: the Mac is out of its box and set up. If you've purchased a Macintosh yourself, follow the "Getting Started" instructions that came with the machine to make sure that the keyboard, mouse, and (if you need one) external monitor are connected. If you are coming to an existing Macintosh in an office, the Mac is probably already set up by its previous owner or the nearest Macintosh guru. This book assumes that the Macintosh has System Software Version 7.0 or later (all Macs coming from the factory since October 1991 are ready to go; ask the guru if you're not sure). That's all. You don't even have to know how to turn on the machine—I cover that soon.

Now, let's cut the malarkey and get on with it. After all, you have a job to do, and all this computer stuff is taking up valuable time.

1st Encounter

The Keyboard

Goal

Gain familiarity with Macintosh keyboard, especially getting the feel of frequently used two-key combinations.

What You Will Need

Place keyboard (or opened PowerBook) in front of you with computer turned off.

Terms of Enfearment

Tab key   Control key
numeric keypad   Option key
function keys   modifier keys
cursor keys   Escape key
Return key   Command key
Enter key

Briefing

In this encounter, we look at the overall layout of Macintosh keyboards and some keys you may have never heard of before.

Keyboard Layout(s)

If you are using a Macintosh with a separate keyboard (i.e., not a portable Mac), you have one of two keyboard styles before you: either the Apple Keyboard (see fig. 1.1) or the Apple Extended Keyboard (see fig. 1.2). Both are perfectly fine for doing day-to-day work with the Mac, but the Extended keyboard includes several keys that provide speedy shortcuts—*speedcuts*—for anyone who does lots of word processing or spreadsheet work.

Figure 1.1
The standard Apple keyboard.

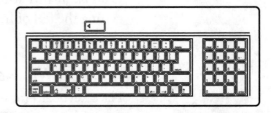

Figure 1.2
The Apple Extended keyboard.

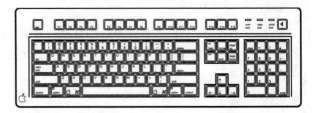

The largest grouping of keys are sometimes collectively called the typewriter keys, because the letters, numbers, *Tab*, and several other keys are placed in the same locations as on any standard typewriter. As you see shortly, some other non-traditional keys are also in this grouping. PowerBook users have little more than these typewriter keys in their laps (see fig. 1.3).

Figure 1.3
*The PowerBook
keyboard.*

To the right edge of both detached keyboards is a *numeric keypad*: a group of keys resembling those found on a simple calculator (see fig. 1.4). If your job entails working with lots of numbers, the numeric keypad will be in constant use. A raised dot on the 5 key helps you keep your hand in position when you can't watch the keyboard during rapid number entry (see fig. 1.5).

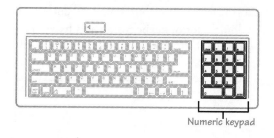

Numeric keypad

Figure 1.4
The numeric keypad.

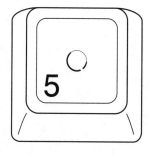

Figure 1.5
*The 5 key on the
numeric keypad has
a raised dot.*

For competitive marketing purposes, Apple had to design the Extended keyboard to the specifications of what was an entrenched standard in the mid 1980s. Therefore, this keyboard features a number of keys and lights that are little used, if at all, in typical Macintosh work. For example, across the top of the Extended keyboard, labeled F1 through F15, are *function keys* (see fig. 1.6). Used heavily on other types of computers, function keys primarily attract dust on Mac keyboards.

Figure 1.6
*The Extended
keyboard function
keys.*

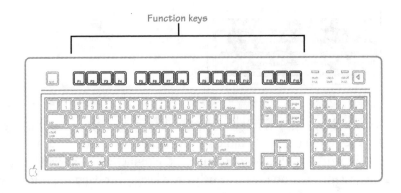

More useful, however, are the home, end, page up, and page down keys (see fig. 1.7). Different software programs react to these four keys differently, but they can be speedcuts when you're doing a lot of keyboarding and have to move quickly from place to place within a document.

Figure 1.7
*The home, page up,
page down, and end
keys.*

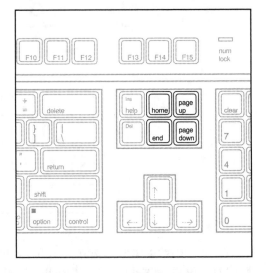

All Mac keyboards have four arrow keys. These keys also are called *cursor keys,* because they control the motion of a cursor on-screen. The Extended keyboard lays out these keys differently than other Mac keyboards (see fig. 1.8). It's murder getting hooked on these keys and then switching between keyboard types. Feel free to heap any annoyance you have with this on the keyboards' designers.

Extended keyboard

Figure 1.8
Cursor key layouts.

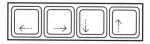

Apple and PowerBook
keyboards

Return and Enter Keys

Virtually every electric typewriter made in the last 20 years (and longer for office models) has a key at the right of the keyboard that positions the carriage (or type ball) to begin typing at the left margin of the next line. In that location on the Macintosh keyboard is the *Return key* (see fig. 1.9). Most software programs respond to a press of the Return key just as the old electric typewriter did.

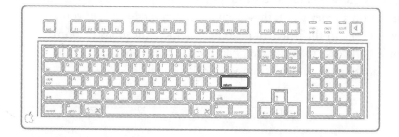

Figure 1.9
The Return key.

Some programs also respond to another key called the *Enter key* (on the numeric keypad if you have one; otherwise the small key to the right of the space bar). I'll have more to say about the differences between Return and Enter in a later encounter, but for now, be aware where these two keys are on your keyboard (see fig. 1.10).

Figure 1.10
Enter key locations.

Keyboards with
numeric keypads

PowerBooks

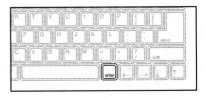

Special Keys

Let's focus on three special keys along the bottom row of the typewriter keys: *Control, Option,* and one with two symbols (and) on it (see fig. 1.11). On the Extended keyboard, a complete set of three graces each side of the space bar. As a group (which also includes the Shift key, whose typical action is the same as on a typewriter), these keys are called *modifier keys*: you hold them down to *modify* the behavior of some other key (or mouse action). This term is fairly easy to remember, because the Shift key modifies the behavior of a letter key to type its uppercase equivalent.

Figure 1.11
*The Control,
Option, and
Command keys.*

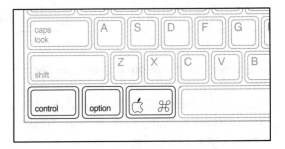

The good news is that you can forget about the Control key. It's a holdover from the olden days of computing and is rarely used in Macintosh software (although sometimes programs enable you to determine its function). The *Escape key* is another old-timer key, which doesn't get much use with the Mac. At best, it may enable you to use the keyboard as an alternative when an opportunity to cancel an operation presents itself on-screen.

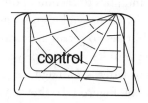

Figure 1.12
The Control and Esc keys on the Macintosh keyboard do little but gather dust.

That leaves the Option and weird symbol keys.

Of the two, the more commonly used one is the one with symbols. In plain language, it's called the *Command key* (see fig. 1.13). Interestingly, the symbol is not referred to in Macintosh terminology, but the ⌘ symbol is. One reason this key is called the Command key is that you can press this key and another key to issue commands telling the Macintosh what to do. These commands are primarily accessible with the mouse, but the Command-key sequence offers a convenient keyboard shortcut, so you don't have to reach for the mouse or trackball to issue a quick command (see fig. 1.14).

Figure 1.13
The Command key.

Figure 1.14
Pressing the Command key and the P key is the same as selecting the Print command with the mouse.

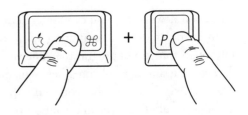

The *Option key* also modifies the action of other keys. Its primary function is to give you access to letters or symbols not found on the keyboard. Just like holding down the Shift key to get an uppercase version of a letter, holding down the Option key enables you to type yet a different character (see fig. 1.15). Sometimes, this letter is a foreign language version of the character; sometimes it's a symbol. Figure 1.16 shows typical characters produced by (a) the normal keyboard, (b) the Shifted keyboard, (c) the Optioned keyboard, and (d) the Shift-Optioned keyboard—sometimes modifier keys need to be ganged up to get the desired results.

Figure 1.15
Pressing the Option key and the P key together produces the character π.

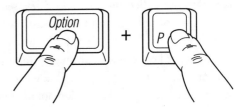

Different from DOS

The Extended keyboard should be familiar to any IBM compatible-computer user: it's the same layout that was made famous (and a world standard) by IBM and its Personal Computer AT model. Using the abridged versions of keyboards may be frustrating at first when you look for the equivalent of the PgUp or PgDn keys. But, hey, you can always get an Extended keyboard (even connect one to your PowerBook).

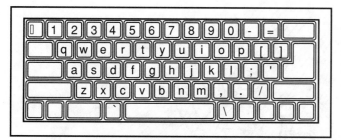

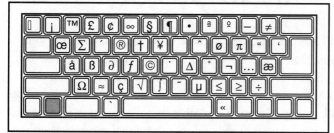

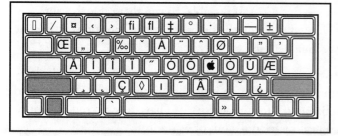

Figure 1.16
Using the Option key enables you to produce many different characters.

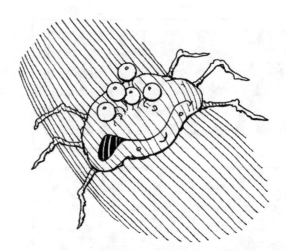

They're Out To Get Us

Apple detached keyboards are very durable. They generally survive soda drenchings, animal hair infestations, and more dust than you would really like to see. The most vulnerable spot, however, is the cable linking the keyboard to the Macintosh (PowerBook owners don't have to worry about this). When no key works, suspect the cable first. Be sure that it's plugged in securely to one side of the keyboard and to a rear panel connector with the ⌘ symbol on it (see fig. 1.17). If possible, try another cable, because keyboard cables can go bad from being bent in weird positions or kept at sharp angles over long periods.

If only a single key isn't working, you know the problem is with the keyboard. Unfortunately, even though it usually means that one switch inside the keyboard is bad, most repair facilities will have to swap out the entire keyboard—for a healthy fee if it's out of warranty.

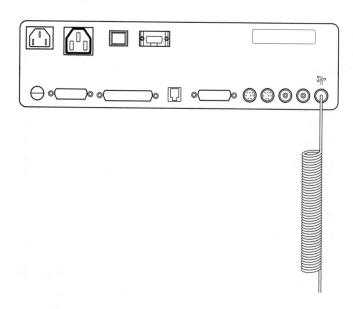

Figure 1.17
*The keyboard should
be plugged into the
ADB port.*

Practice

The Return Key

With the computer off, play with typing fictional information into fictional
software just to get the feel for the rhythms of entering computer information.

Enter the following information in a column, pressing the Return key after
each name (see fig. 1.18):

Adams (Return)
Bacon (Return)
Camus (Return)
Dante (Return)
Eliot (Return)
Faulkner (Return)
Gibbon (Return)
Hardy (Return)
Ibsen (Return)

James (Return)
Kafka (Return)
Lawrence (Return)

Figure 1.18
*A printout of the
Return key exorcise.*

Adams

Bacon

Camus

Dante

Eliot

Faulkner

Gibbon

Hardy

Ibsen

James

Kafka

Lawrence

The Tab Key

Enter the following information in a three-column format, with tabs after the first and second names and a Return at the end of the line:

Last (Tab) First (Tab) Title (Return)
Machiavelli (Tab) Niccolo (Tab) The Prince (Return)
Nietzche (Tab) Friedrich (Tab) Beyond Good and Evil (Return)
O'Neill (Tab) Eugene (Tab) Mourning Becomes Electra (Return)
Paine (Tab) Thomas (Tab) The Age of Reason (Return)
Rabelais (Tab) Francois (Tab) Gargantua and Pantagruel (Return)
Santayana (Tab) George (Tab) Scepticism and Animal Faith (Return)
Thackeray (Tab) William (Tab) Vanity Fair (Return)
Virgil (Tab) Publius (Tab) The Aeneid (Return)
Wells (Tab) H.G. (Tab) The Time Machine (Return)
Yeats (Tab) William Butler (Tab) The Prelude (Return)
Zola (Tab) Emile (Tab) Germinal (Return)

Last	First	Title
Machiavelli	Niccolo	The Prince
Nietzche	Friedrich	Beyond Good and Evil
O'Neill	Eugene	Mourning Becomes Electra
Paine	Thomas	The Age of Reason
Rabelais	Francois	Gargantua and Pantagruel
Santayana	George	Scpeticism and Animal Faith
Thackeray	William	Vanity Fair
Virgil	Publius	The Aeneid
Wells	H.G.	The Time Machine
Yeats	William Butler	The Prelude
Zola	Emile	Germinal

Figure 1.19
A printout of the Tab key exorcise.

The Command Key

Common commands issued with the Command key are Command-S, Command-Q, Command-C, and Command-V, all of which are on the left side of the keyboard. Developing a one-handed technique is valuable (but not crucial).

1. Issue a Command-S with your left hand by pressing the Command key with your thumb and the S key with your left index finger.

2. Say "Command-S" aloud to associate the physical action with the command.

3. Release all keys and cycle through these four commands (Command-S, -Q, -C, and -V) at least 10 times, saying the word "Command" and the letter out loud as you press the letter.

The Option Key

1. In earlier practice, one of the names was Francois. Technically, it should be spelled François, which you can do easily on the Macintosh. The special ç character is made possible by holding down the Option

key and pressing the C key. Type each of the following words five times, using the Option-key equivalent:

a. François

b. garçon

2. A common symbol folks like to use in Macintosh documents is the bullet (•), which is produced by typing Option-8. Type the following indented, bulleted list five times to feel the rhythm:

Option-8 First Return
Tab Option-8 Second Return
Tab Tab Option-8 Third Return

Figure 1.20
A printout of the Option key exorcise.

• First
    • Second
        • Third

Summary

In this encounter, you've seen how the basic layout of Macintosh keyboards combine familiar typewriter keyboards, calculator keyboards, and some special keys. Two of those special keys, the Option and Command keys, play important roles in using the Macintosh productively. Moreover, the imposing array of keys on the Extended keyboard isn't so frightening because most of the extra keys go unused in Macintosh operations.

Exorcises

1. Which symbol does the Macintosh use to represent the Command key?

   a. ⇧

   b.

   c.

   d. ⌘

   e.

2. Based on your knowledge of what the Shift key does, which of the following symbols could represent that key?

   a. ⇧

   b. ⟨X⟩

   c. ◆

   d. ⌘

   e.

3. The Shift, Option, Command, and Control keys as a group are called _____ keys, because _____.

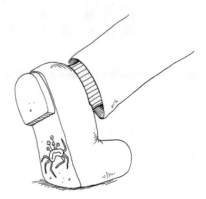

2nd Encounter

Turning on
the Macintosh

Goal

Learn the proper way to switch on your Macintosh and know if the machine is starting properly.

What You Will Need

Computer turned off.

Terms of Enfearment

booting
dialog box
startup
Desktop
icon

Briefing

Finding the Switch

The first time you sit before your Macintosh, it may not be clear how to turn the darned thing on. After all, there's no big ON/OFF or Power switch staring you in the face. The way you turn the machine on differs among several classes of Macintosh models.

Most low- and mid-priced Macintosh models (current models include the Performa 200, 400 series, Classic II, LC series, and Centris series) do, in fact, have a big rocker-type switch, but it's on the rear of the computer (see fig. 2.1). Reach around (the left side for some models, the right side for others) and press the top half of the switch until the switch snaps to the on position.

Figure 2.1

The on/off switch is located on the back of Performa 200, Performa 400 series, Classic II, LC series, and Centris series machines.

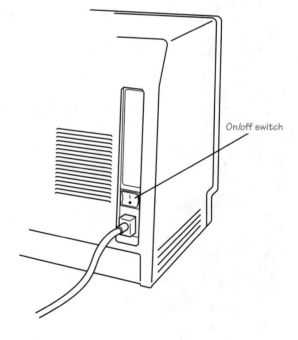

On/off switch

All other desktop models make switching on easier by letting us do it from the keyboard. On the Apple and Extended keyboards is a switch with a left facing triangle; naturally, they're in different places and of different sizes on either keyboard style (see fig. 2.2). As long as the keyboard is connected, we can touch this key to turn on the machine. Because most external video monitors can be plugged into the Macintosh system unit, it is more convenient if we turn the monitor's power switch on and leave it on. Thus, turning the computer on and off does the same for the monitor, and it's one less power switch to worry about from here on.

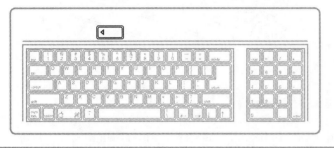

Figure 2.2
Keyboard "on" switch locations.

How we switch on portable Macs also varies somewhat from model to model. It is always best to try touching any character key (the space bar is usually the most convenient) to see whether the machine starts up that way. If nothing happens, you will have to open the trap door on the rear panel and press the power button.

Figure 2.3
*The PowerBook
power button.*

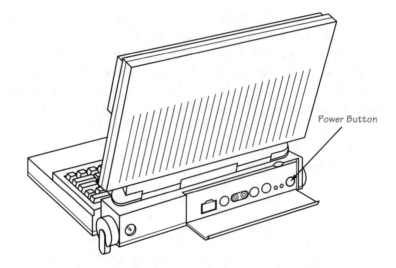

Power Button

What Happens Next?

Getting the computer to begin doing its thing is known by a couple of jargon terms. The most arcane is called *booting* the computer. No, not like kicking it in the butt with your boot. The term derives from the more formal term bootstrap, which, in turn, came from the idea that the hunk of wires and components pulls itself up by its bootstraps to start acting like a computer. In Macintosh terms, the action of turning on the machine is called *startup*—how simple.

After you turn on the machine, it goes through an automatic process that can last a minute or so (see fig. 2.4). The first task it performs is a quick check of some of the machine's innards. If everything is OK, you hear a tone or chord come through the speaker. You want to hear this sound every time.

Next, you should see a small picture of a Macintosh in the center of your video screen. This picture is called an *icon*—you'll see lots of icons while using the Macintosh. If a smiling face appears in the icon, you know that the machine has located additional software (on a floppy or hard disk) to continue starting up.

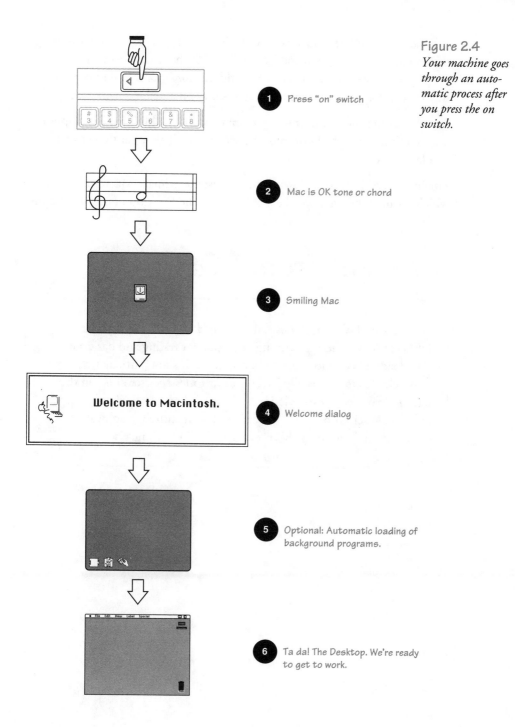

1. Press "on" switch

2. Mac is OK tone or chord

3. Smiling Mac

Welcome to Macintosh.

4. Welcome dialog

5. Optional: Automatic loading of background programs.

6. Ta da! The Desktop. We're ready to get to work.

Figure 2.4
Your machine goes through an automatic process after you press the on switch.

After a few seconds, the icon is replaced by what looks like a banner bearing the comforting words, Welcome to Macintosh. The white area with the message is known in the Macintosh world as a *dialog box*, in that it is one way for the computer to communicate—carry on a dialog—with you.

As the startup process continues, you may see some additional icons appear one at a time along the bottom of the screen. We'll see what these icons are in a later encounter.

Finally, everything settles down, and you see the primary Macintosh screen, which is called the *Desktop*. We'll learn about the Desktop in the next lesson.

Different from DOS

Few desktop DOS machines can be turned on from the keyboard. DOS computers, too, go through component testing and basic software loading sequences during booting, but it's not particularly pretty to watch. There are usually streams of text messages scrolling on the screen as you see in excruciating and superfluous detail what is happening. The Macintosh, on the other hand, is an entirely graphical presentation in not only this process, but in everything else.

They're Out To Get Us

The startup process on a Macintosh is perhaps the most likely place in which you'll encounter problems that seem insurmountable. The problems will be due to things as innocuous as a loose cable to the extremely rare yet harrowing damaged hard disk. I've reserved a special encounter (20) on how to diagnose and get help for such problems.

When absolutely nothing happens, look to the obvious problem that electric power is not reaching the Mac. Either the power cable isn't connected, or it's plugged into a power outlet that doesn't have power (perhaps the outlet is controlled by a light switch that is off). Also check the keyboard cable (see the 1st Encounter) if that's where the power-on key is for your Macintosh model.

If you've just purchased your Macintosh and it doesn't start, make it the responsibility of the seller (be it dealer or individual) to make sure that the machine is functioning properly. Or, if you're in a corporate environment, contact the technical support person for help in making sure that the computer turns on properly. Lastly, if you're stuck with no one to turn to for help, you can jump ahead to the first part of the 20th Encounter and try working your way through. Chances are that the problem for a newly acquired machine is a simple one that won't be technically taxing.

Practice

Power On, Dude

For the 99.99 percent of you who are working your way through this lesson, your Macintosh will turn on properly. It's important that you listen and watch carefully as the startup process progresses.

1. If your Macintosh has an external video monitor, turn its power switch on. If the monitor's power cord is plugged into the Macintosh system unit, nothing should happen yet.

2. Using the "Briefing" as a guide, locate, *but do not yet press*, the power switch for your Macintosh.

3. With all your senses poised for input, press the power switch and watch the screen carefully.

4. Unless you already know how to turn off your Macintosh from previous experience, leave it on for the next few encounters (they won't take long).

Summary

We've learned how to start up a Macintosh and have seen a few elements important to Macintosh work—icons and dialog boxes—of which we'll see plenty in the next encounters.

Exorcises

1. After you switch on the Macintosh, it goes through a process known as the _____ process. Computer oldtimers may also call this action _____ the computer.

2. A small picture on the screen that represents an object of some kind is called a(n) _____.

3. Place a number next to each item in the following list in the order that they occur after you switch on your Macintosh:

   _____ "Welcome to Macintosh" dialog box

   _____ Smiling Macintosh icon

   _____ Icons appear across bottom of screen

   _____ Desktop appears

   _____ Startup tone or chord sounds

What You See on the Screen

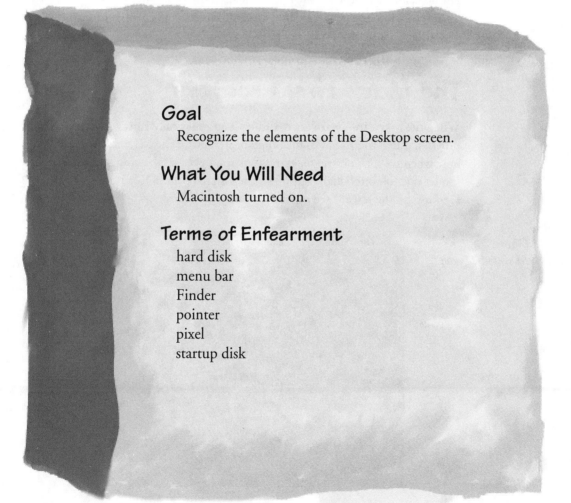

Goal
Recognize the elements of the Desktop screen.

What You Will Need
Macintosh turned on.

Terms of Enfearment
hard disk
menu bar
Finder
pointer
pixel
startup disk

Briefing

The Macintosh "remembers" things from session to session because all
information you type or draw is stored on the device known as the *hard disk*.
Yes, it actually rotates like a record or compact disc and is capable of storing
a large amount of information in a relatively small space. A future encounter
will explore what's actually on the hard disk and how we manage stuff on it.
For now, all we need to know is that the hard disk is an important repository
for information and programs that let the Macintosh act as a word processor,
spreadsheet, or whatever else we want it to do.

The Mac's First Program

When the Macintosh starts successfully, it automatically runs a special
program called the *Finder*. This program starts with the Macintosh and stops
only when we turn off the machine. We don't even see most of what the
Finder does on our behalf, but one quite visible thing it does is present the
Desktop on the screen (see fig. 3.1).

Figure 3.1
Macintosh Desktop.

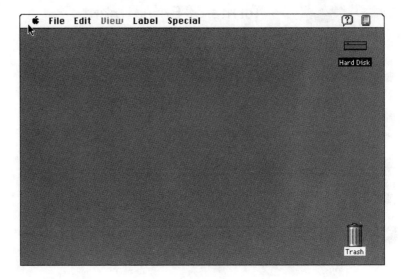

Like the surface of a physical desk, the Desktop is our workspace for all our Macintosh work. Regard the underlying pattern (dots or gray on a factory fresh Macintosh) as the surface of the desktop (see fig. 3.2). It may not be oak or rosewood, but it means as much business as any executive desktop we'll ever see.

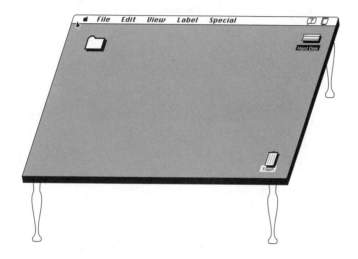

Figure 3.2
The Macintosh Desktop is like any business executive's desktop.

Giant Mosaic

If you look at the screen closely for a second, you may see that everything on the Desktop is nothing more than a careful positioning of nearly microscopic squares (see fig. 3.3). Each tiny point is called a picture element— *pixel* for short. The size of your Desktop is measured not in inches, but by the number of pixels horizontally by the number vertically. Remembering the actual numbers for your Mac model isn't important, but as a means of reference, the smallest Desktop is found on the Classic and Performa 200 types of machines: 512-by-342 pixels; PowerBook screens are 640 pixels across by 400 down (see fig. 3.4). The greater the number of pixels to your Desktop, the more stuff you can put on it, up to some giant external monitors capable of displaying 1,664 pixels across by 1,200 down.

Figure 3.3

*The file folder icon
consists of many
pixels (normal size is
at right).*

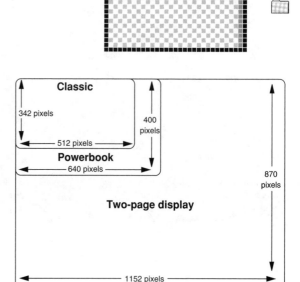

Figure 3.4

*Comparative
Macintosh screen
sizes.*

Desktop Elements

Across the top of the screen (floating between the Desktop and our eye) is the *menu bar.* I'll cover this topic in detail in the 5th Encounter. Suffice it to say that the menu bar is where we issue commands to make many things happen.

Because it is usually vital to point to something on the Macintosh screen to issue a command or say the equivalent of "I want to work with this thing here," a *pointer* is always visible on the screen (see fig. 3.6). In the next encounter, we'll see how to control that pointer.

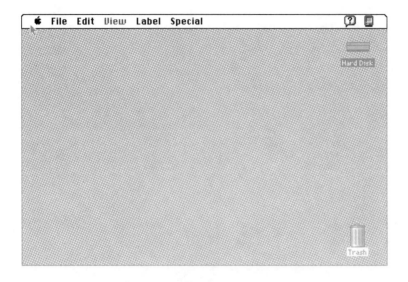

Figure 3.5
The menu bar atop the Macintosh Desktop.

Figure 3.6
Screen pointer atop an icon.

Icons also grace the Desktop. Near the top right corner is a representation of the hard disk as an icon. If your Desktop has more than one hard disk icon, the topmost one is the one that started the Macintosh (it is called the *startup disk*). The design of a hard disk icon can vary, but the standard icon that comes with Macs from the factory is shown in figure 3.7. Every hard disk has a name, which you are free to change to suit your whim (8th Encounter).

The other prominent icon on the Desktop is labeled Trash (see fig. 3.8). Although you may not have a trash can on top of your physical desk, the Macintosh has one on its Desktop—kind of like the Waste receptacle on a writing table at the bank.

Figure 3.7
The Hard Disk icon.

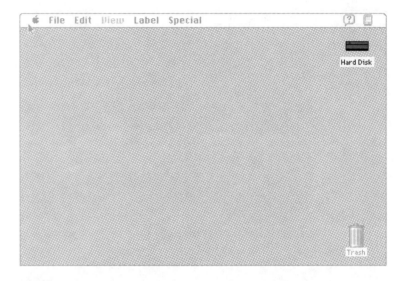

Figure 3.8
The Trash icon.

When the Mac starts up, one or more windows may also open. We'll skip over these for the moment, because they become more important later.

Performa owners note: You also probably see a window and icon called *Launcher*. Don't worry about these for now. You'll be able to read about them later in your *Macintosh User's Guide*.

What Finder Does

The Finder program runs all the time to help us organize information in our hard disk directly or through other programs, as we'll see later. For example, in the real world, if we want ready access to a folder of information, we may leave the folder out on our desk, so we don't have to go rummaging through a file drawer to get it later. Similarly, the Finder lets us leave out on the Desktop items normally stored away in our hard disk (see fig. 3.9). The free-form way the Macintosh Finder lets us work with familiar stuff is one reason many people like the Macintosh and find it comparatively easy to learn.

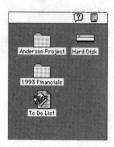

Figure 3.9
Frequently used folders and documents located conveniently on the Desktop.

Different from DOS

The Desktop is one of the biggest shocks to anyone coming to the Macintosh from DOS. Unless you've used Windows, the concept of looking at your hard disk's contents in any way other than a directory

continues

> listing is unsettling. Initially, the Finder may even feel restricting. Over time, however, you will discover that the Finder tells you a great deal about your computer at a quick glance, and you may wonder how you suffered with the old directory listing.

They're Out To Get Us

If anything is going to confuse you about your first explorations around the Desktop, it will be caused by someone else who has been fiddling around with that particular Macintosh. The hard disk may be divided into more than one section, each with its own icon. In a corporate environment, the Macintosh may have started up and automatically connected to another Macintosh or computer elsewhere in the office. That other computer (called a file server) will also have an icon on the Desktop with some little cables running in and out of it to show that it's wired to a network (see fig. 3.10).

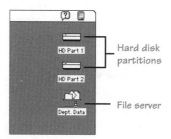

Figure 3.10
Desktop with a hard disk divided into two volumes plus a file server volume from the network.

Someone may have also altered the Desktop pattern. Although the Macintosh allows easy Desktop pattern selections from a preset library (see the 16th Encounter), it is equally possible that a custom pattern has been put into your machine. Don't worry; the Desktop pattern is strictly decorative. One pattern won't make your Mac work better than another, but a crazy pattern may make it harder to pick out icons, so your choice can affect your interaction with the Mac (see fig. 3.11).

Figure 3.11
Weird Desktop patterns can make icons hard to find.

A previous user may have also left a number of icons to programs, documents, and folders out on the Desktop. Until we learn how to organize these things, don't worry about them. We'll straighten things up later.

When you talk to experienced Macintosh users, you will encounter the terms Desktop and Finder used interchangeably. Technically, the Desktop is a *place*, and the Finder is a *program*. They are heavily interrelated, however, so don't be thrown off track by improper use—and don't worry if you use the terms incorrectly. Other Mac users will know what you mean.

Practice

Getting To Know You

In this get-acquainted encounter, you'll simply use your finger to point to each of the major elements that the Finder presents to the screen and say its name aloud. Point at (but keep your finger off the screen if you can) the items shown in the following list and say their names. Go through all items until you can point to all five items and name them without referring to figure 3.12.

Desktop
menu bar
pointer
hard disk
trash

Figure 3.12
The parts of the Macintosh screen.

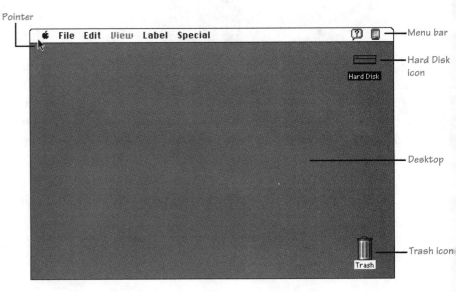

Summary

I introduced the Finder and its Desktop display elements. These are important building blocks for working with the Mac minute-by-minute.

Exorcises

1. The program that runs when we start the Macintosh is called
   _____.

2. A hallmark of the Macintosh display is its real-world metaphor to a
   _____, which, by no surprise on the Macintosh is called
   _____.

3. Upon close examination, the Macintosh screen consists of dots called
   _____.

4. Match the item names to the callouts in the Macintosh screen illustration in figure 3.13:
   a) hard disk
   b) menu bar
   c) pointer
   d) Desktop
   e) Finder

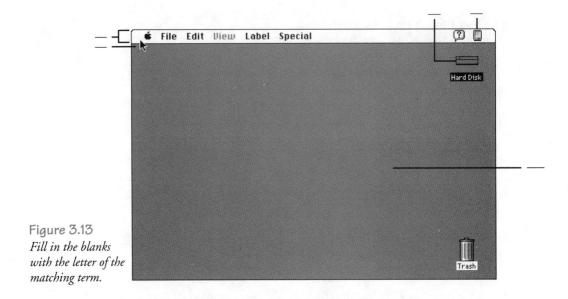

Figure 3.13
*Fill in the blanks
with the letter of the
matching term.*

Getting Used to the Mouse or Trackball

Goal

Gain confidence and coordination controlling the
pointer with the mouse or trackball; understand the
use of the mouse button and standard mouse actions.

What You Will Need

Macintosh computer turned on.

Terms of Enfearment

mouse
trackball
mouse button
clicking
selecting
dragging
drag-and-drop
double-click

Briefing

When the Macintosh was introduced in 1984, it was the first mass-produced personal computer to come with a *mouse* as standard equipment (see fig. 4.1). Previously used only on very expensive computers for special graphics purposes, the mouse—a cigarette-pack sized device tethered to the computer—is as important to controlling the computer as the keyboard.

Figure 4.1

A typical Macintosh mouse.

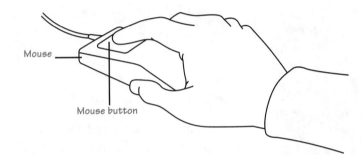

Mouse

Mouse button

On PowerBooks, the mouse is supplanted by a built-in device—the *trackball*—that gives you full mouse functionality without having to worry about a cable or desk space to use the mouse (see fig. 4.2). Despite the plethora of laptop computer designs in the world, the PowerBook is the first to place the trackball squarely in front of the user in a design that makes so much sense for typical portable operation that it's amazing no one else had thought of it before.

Underneath a Macintosh mouse is a little roller ball, which rotates as you move the mouse around the physical desk (see fig. 4.3). The roller must touch the desk—the minute you pick up the mouse, you cut off the mouse's legs. If the desk is slippery, a mousepad will help the ball maintain good traction. With a trackball, you more directly manipulate the roller ball (with your thumb or forefinger), but the operating principle for both devices is the same. From here on, I just refer to all of this as using the mouse.

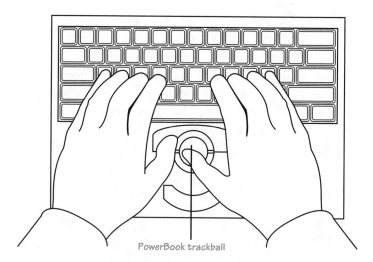

PowerBook trackball

Figure 4.2
The PowerBook trackball.

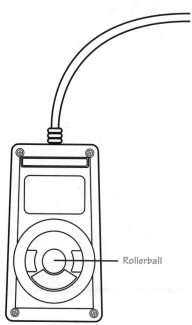

Rollerball

Figure 4.3
Underneath the mouse.

Moving the Screen Pointer

In the last encounter, you saw the pointer on-screen. The mouse is what you use to move the pointer around the screen. The direction of pointer movement corresponds to the direction in which you move the mouse: in straight lines, diagonals, or even circles (see fig. 4.4). The Macintosh doesn't let you move the pointer entirely off the screen. If you should lose sight of the pointer, jiggle the mouse a bit until you see something—the pointer—move.

Figure 4.4

Pointer motion on the screen desktop is identical to mouse motion on the physical desk.

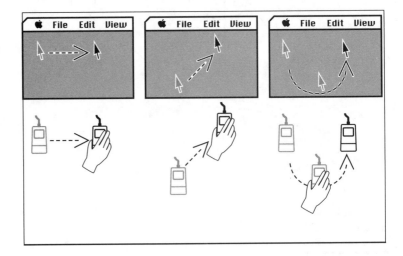

The most effective way to hold the mouse is to cover it with your hand so that it fills your palm; your thumb should be against one side, and your middle, ring, and pinkie fingers should grab the other side. Your index finger should be free to rest atop the rectangle near the mouse cord. This area is called the *mouse button* (see fig. 4.1 again). You use your index finger to press down and release the mouse button—an action called *clicking*—as shown in figure 4.5. (You usually can hear an internal switch click when you press and release the button.)

Figure 4.5
Clicking the mouse button.

PowerBook trackballs appear to have two buttons, above and below the ball. In truth, both buttons act the same way. Which button you use is more a question of personal preference than dictate. Here are some possibilities:

▪ Keep most fingers on the keyboard; use thumb for ball and upper button.

▪ Use thumb for ball; use index finger for upper button.

▪ Use thumb of one hand for ball; use thumb of other for upper button.

▪ Shift hand toward you slightly and use thumb on lower button while rolling ball with index finger (see fig. 4.6).

▪ Any combination of all the above depending on the action you intend.

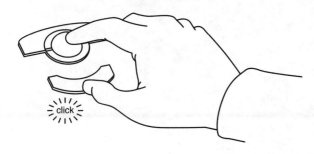

Figure 4.6
One hand position for the trackball that makes clicking and rolling easy.

Clicking the Mouse Button

Just moving the pointer around the screen usually doesn't invoke any actions. That's what the mouse button is for.

If you position the pointer atop an icon on the Desktop and click the mouse button, something usually happens. Most commonly, the icon you clicked becomes active as shown in figure 4.7 (it changes color or turns black, depending on your screen). This is how you select one item from all the others on the Desktop so that you can issue some command to affect that item. When an instruction tells you to click on an item, position the pointer atop the item, press the mouse button, and release it. Highlighting an item like this also is called *selecting* the item. The next instruction you give probably acts on that selected item.

Figure 4.7
The results of clicking on (selecting) the Hard Disk icon.

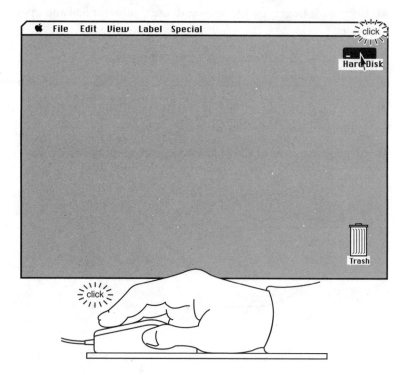

On a Roll

The next important action you can accomplish with the mouse is a combination of two actions I've already covered: clicking the mouse (holding the mouse button down) *and* moving the mouse and its pointer (see fig. 4.8). Contrary to the old joke, even people who deem themselves as uncoordinated *can* chew gum and walk at the same time. The action here is no more complex than holding and sliding an object across a table without picking it up. The formal term for this action is *clicking and dragging*—or just dragging (which assumes, correctly, that you can't drag an item unless you have clicked and held it first). And, it's far easier than rubbing your tummy and patting your head at the same time.

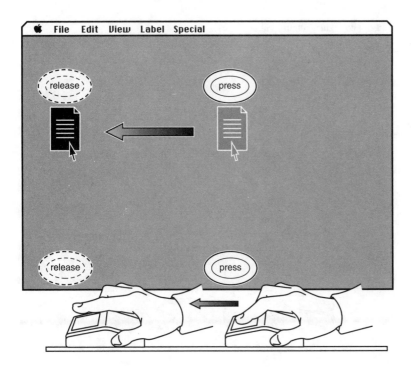

Figure 4.8
Clicking on a document icon and dragging it to the left.

In addition to just moving things around by clicking and dragging, some actions you can take with icons involve dragging one item to another item. Figure 4.9 shows the action of clicking on a document icon, dragging it across the screen, and dropping it on a folder icon. As you will see in later encounters, this is one way to get a document into a folder. It's magic compared to real life, because it lets us essentially drag a document on top of a folder, and the document zips inside the folder. We can tell if this *drag-and-drop* action will work for something, because not only is the dragged object highlighted, but when we drag it atop its destination, the destination icon also highlights—meaning that it is ready to accept the drop (i.e., release of the mouse button). The drag-and-drop concept is gaining popularity in Macintosh programs.

Figure 4.9
Drag-and-dropping a document icon.

Document Icon

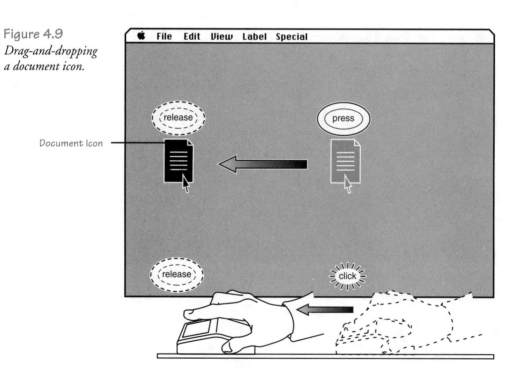

The last mouse action I cover here—the *double click*—is actually a shortcut to otherwise laborious actions. A double-click consists of nothing more than two quickly spaced clicks of the mouse button. A double-click atop a desktop icon is generally the way to bring that icon alive. For example, double-clicking on a hard disk icon zooms open that disk so that you see some or all of its contents (see fig. 4.10); double-clicking on a folder opens up that folder. Double-clicking on an icon representing a document opens that document (and the program required to view or change the document). All of these actions could be carried out more laboriously by single click-ing—selecting—the icon and then issuing a command from the menu bar. Double-clicking is much faster and should become natural to you in a short time.

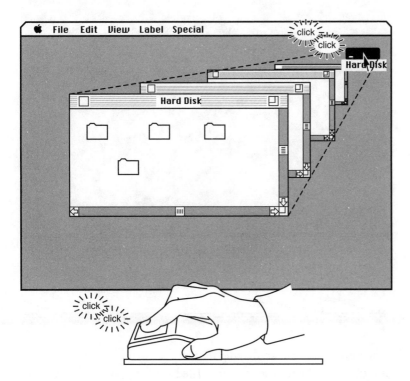

Figure 4.10
Double-clicking the hard disk icon opens the disk so that you can view the contents.

How quickly the mouse and buttons respond to your actions is modifiable. You learn more about this in the 16th Encounter but take comfort in knowing that you can adjust how quickly the pointer reacts to rolling the mouse.

The Mouse and Desk Space

Early mousers will encounter those moments when there isn't enough desk to finish moving the pointer or dragging an item on-screen. Remember that the pointer responds to motion of the little roller under the mouse. If you pick up the mouse and wave it in the air, the roller doesn't move, so the pointer doesn't either. Therefore, you can literally pick up the mouse from the desk surface and place it where you have more space to finish the movement (see fig. 4.11).

Figure 4.11

Lifting the mouse from the desk does not move the on-screen pointer.

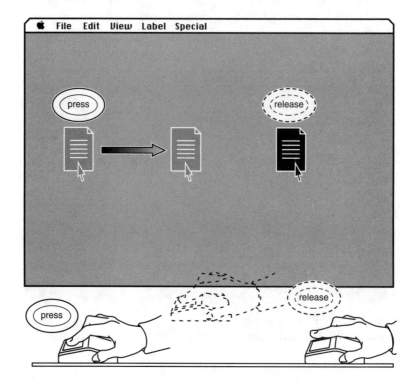

If you find, however, that you are having to pick up the mouse a lot, you probably should adjust the mouse motion (called *tracking*), which I cover in the 16th Encounter.

Different from DOS

DOS programs at best offer mouse control as an option. Hardly any IBM-clone computers ship with a mouse, so a program designer has to assume a common denominator that does not include a mouse. Mice for PCs have two buttons. No standard exists for what the second button should do in a program, even under Windows. Many Macintosh users who have switched from DOS or Windows believe that the Macintosh pointer motion is smoother and more coordinated with the hand motion of the mouse.

They're Out To Get Us

When the mouse doesn't seem to work, a couple of things could be wrong. The simplest possibility is that the mouse isn't connected properly. Macintosh keyboards have an extra jack for the mouse plug to give you plenty of rope with which to hang the mouse with (see fig. 4.12). This means that the keyboard must be connected properly as well. A frozen pointer also may mean that the computer has frozen. See the 20th Encounter about this unfortunate event.

Figure 4.12
The mouse is plugged into the keyboard, which is plugged into the Apple Desktop Bus port on the back of the Macintosh.

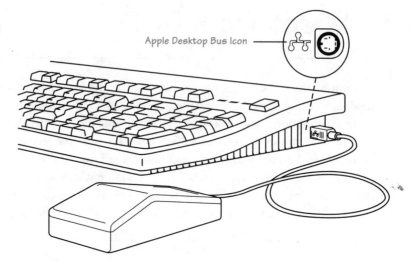

Apple Desktop Bus Icon

Mouse and trackball innards can get dirty (animal hair is a primary enemy), and the balls may not spin freely or smoothly. If this happens, you need to remove and clean the roller balls as described in the *Macintosh User's Guide* that came with your machine.

One final gotcha to watcha is the drag-and-drop that missed. It's easy enough to do: you drag one item to another; the destination highlights; but before you actually release the mouse button to affect the drop, you drag a little further to unhighlight the destination. The result is the dragged item sitting almost atop the destination icon in a jumbled mess (see fig. 4.13). It's simple enough to fix: just drag the item a few pixels and drop it again. No harm either way.

Figure 4.13
Missing the destination of a drag-and-drop action results in overlapping icons. Try again.

OOPS! Missed the target

Practice

Roll, Roll, Roll Your Mouse...

Get the feel of how the pointer responds to the mouse or trackball movement by performing the following pointer motions:

1. Move the pointer a couple of inches on the screen back and forth horizontally.

2. Do the same vertically.

3. Try moving the pointer a short distance along a diagonal.

4. With the pointer on the left side of the screen, slowly move the mouse or trackball until the pointer is touching the right side of the screen. If you are using a mouse and run out of desk space, pick up the mouse and position it back on the left of the space to continue the pointer's journey across the screen.

5. With the pointer on the right side of the screen, move the mouse or trackball quickly until the pointer is touching the left side of the screen. How quickly it moves (it may do it in much less space than before) depends on an internal setting you adjust in a later encounter.

Clicking

Now practice single clicking.

1. Click once on the Trash icon. See it highlight.

2. Click once on the Desktop pattern. The previously selected item is no longer selected.

3. Click once on the Trash icon to select it again.

4. Click once on the hard disk icon. The hard disk is now selected, but the Trash is not.

Figure 4.14
The results of your single clicking practice session.

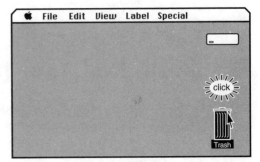

Figure A

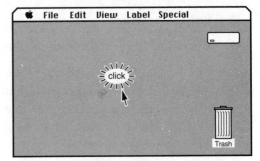

Figure B

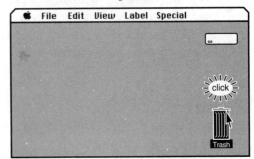

Figure C

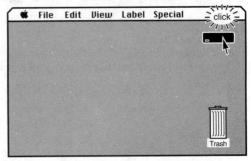

Figure D

Dragging

1. Click and drag the Trash icon from the lower right to a position just to the left of the hard disk icon

2. Click and drag the Trash icon back to the lower right corner (the exact location isn't critical).

Double-Clicking

Double-click the hard disk icon. If no window had been open before, one will zoom out of the icon, revealing several more icons.

Drag-and-Drop

1. Locate an item in this hard disk window other than the one labeled System Folder and drag it from the window out onto the Desktop.

2. Drag that same item near the hard disk icon and keep the mouse button pressed while you slowly drag it onto and away from the hard disk icon. Notice how the hard disk icon highlights when the pointer is atop it.

3. When the hard disk icon is highlighted, release the mouse button, dropping the selected item onto the hard disk icon. This is one way to get that item back into the window.

Summary

By learning the primary actions of the mouse and trackball, you have completed a survey of the physical means of interacting with the computer—including the keyboard from the previous encounter. Important concepts for the mouse include clicking to select an item, dragging an item across the screen, double-clicking an item, and dragging-and-dropping one item onto another.

Exorcises

1. When you click on an item, you also _____ that item.

2. Describe the three primary physical actions involved with dragging an item from one place to another.

3. If you see an icon on the Desktop, what would you do to see what it can do or what it contains?

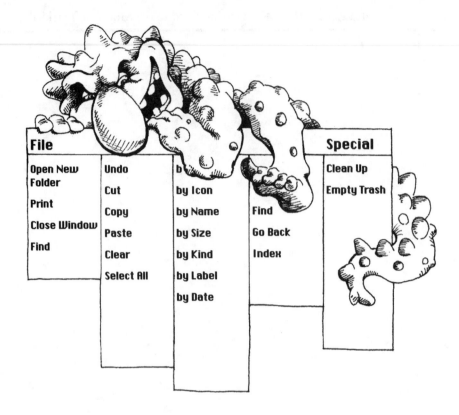

File

Open New
Folder

Print

Close Window

Find

Undo

Cut

Copy

Paste

Clear

Select All

b

by Icon

by Name

by Size

by Kind

by Label

by Date

Find

Go Back

Index

Special

Clean Up

Empty Trash

5th Encounter

Controlling the Machine

Goal

Learn to rely on the menu bar as the first place to look for what to do next.

What You Will Need

Macintosh turned on, showing the Desktop

Terms of Enfearment

pull-down menu   Application menu
Apple menu   dimmed item
File menu   command-key equivalents
Edit menu   hierarchical menus
Help menu

Briefing

You have seen how to get something to happen on the Macintosh screen by double-clicking items or dragging them around. But how do we get down to some real work? What is the machine capable of doing at any given moment?

The primary communication path between us and the Macintosh is via menus—lists of things the Macintosh can do for us now. When you don't know what to do next, the best place to look is through the menus in the hope of finding something that rings a bell.

Macintosh menus are called *pull-down menus*, because we use the mouse to pull them down like window shades from the menu bar across the top of the screen (see fig. 5.1). Each little picture or word in the menu bar is the name of a menu. The leftmost picture, the Apple icon, heads the Apple menu. To its right is the File menu, followed by the Edit menu, and so on (see fig. 5.2).

Figure 5.1
*Pull-down menus
are like window
shades.*

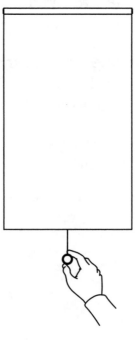

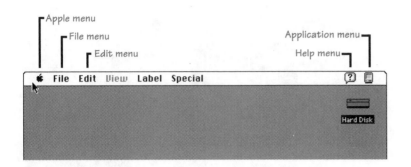

Check Out a Menu

To pull down a menu, summon your click-and-drag experience. First, position the pointer atop the menu name. Then click and hold down the mouse button (see fig. 5.3). As long as you hold down the mouse button and keep the pointer on the menu name, the menu will stay down. Releasing the mouse button while the pointer is still on the menu name causes the menu to roll up, without taking any action. You can use this method to scan down a menu to see whether you recognize a command to select for your next step. In fact, you can scan each menu in turn by dragging slowly along the menu bar (see fig. 5.4). Dragging the pointer to another menu rolls up the first menu and pulls down the next.

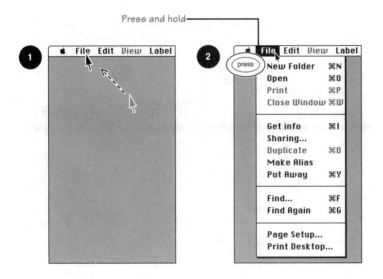

Figure 5.3
Dragging the mouse pointer to the File menu and then clicking and holding down the mouse button pulls down the File menu to view its choices.

Figure 5.4
*Slowly drag across
the menu bar to view
all menus.*

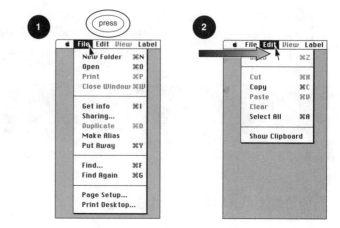

Make a Choice

To select an item in the menu bar, continue holding down the mouse
button while dragging down the menu. As the pointer touches each item in
the menu, that item highlights to confirm which item is currently selected
(see fig. 5.5). You can drag up and down the menu. If the pointer goes
outside the bounds of the pulled down menu, no item will be selected—
releasing the mouse button now is another way to let the menu roll up
without taking any action.

Figure 5.5
*How to choose a
menu item.*

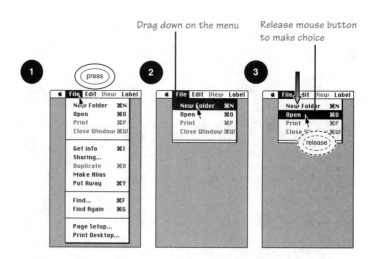

Longer menus, such as the File menu shown in figure 5.6, usually divide items into logical groups. Dividing lines separate the groups.

Figure 5.6
Dividing lines don't respond to the pointer but help visually group related commands to make them easier to find in long lists.

When you find a menu item that you want, make sure that it is selected and release the mouse button. It flashes a few times as a visual reinforcement of the item you selected.

Dot-Dot-Dot...

Not all menu selections take immediate actions when you choose them. When chosen, a menu item that ends with three dots (called an *ellipsis*) displays a dialog box (see fig. 5.7). Such dialog boxes can contain just about anything, but they always have a Cancel button or close box, which enables you to close the dialog box. Closing the box returns you to the exact place you were in before you pulled down the original menu.

Standard Menus

The Macintosh has one menu bar, but its contents change as you shift from program to program (you will see more about this later). A number of menus, however, are always present, even if their contents change from program to program. These menus are the *Apple, File, Edit, Help*, and *Application* menus. The Apple, File, and Edit menus are the first three on the left, and the Help and Application menus hug the right end of the menu bar. Any additional menus (some small programs have no additional menus) appear to the right of the Edit menu (see fig. 5.8). Their names, contents, and functions are determined solely by the program that is active at any given moment.

Figure 5.7
A menu item ending in three dots (ellipsis) always leads to a window in which you can select more actions or choices.

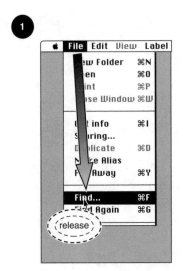

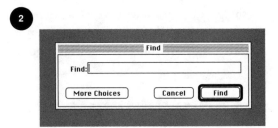

Dim, But Not Dumb

From time to time, you will encounter menus or items in a menu that appear grayed-out. These items are said to be *dimmed* (see fig. 5.9). You can obviously view a dimmed item to see what it says, but in no way can you select it with the pointer. A dimmed item is not available.

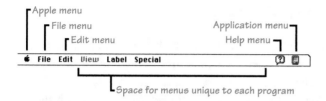

Figure 5.8
Menus between the Edit and Help menus are different for each program.

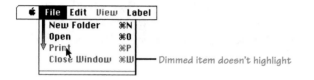

Figure 5.9
A dimmed item in a menu means that it is not active at the moment.

When you see a dimmed item, it means that something else isn't set properly for that menu item to mean anything. For example, in the Finder, if you click on the hard disk icon, the View menu is dimmed. If you then click on the Desktop pattern, the Label menu also dims (see fig. 5.10). You don't have to know what items in the Label menu do to know that they can affect only a selected item in the Finder.

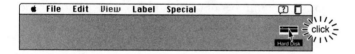

Figure 5.10
The Label menu applies to any selected item in the Desktop. Click in the Desktop pattern, and the Label menu dims, because no relevant item is selected.

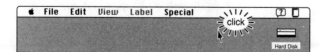

Look Ma, No Mouse!

Many menu commands can be activated from the keyboard, rather than requiring the mouse to choose them. Menu items followed by the command key symbol (⌘) and a letter have *command-key equivalents*. By holding down the Command key and the other character key, you accomplish the same as pulling down the menu with the mouse, selecting the item, and releasing the mouse button. In fact, you usually see the menu name highlight whenever you issue one of these command-key equivalents. Command-key equivalents are provided expressly as speedcuts.

Figure 5.11
Pressing the Command key and the P key at the same time issues the Print command.

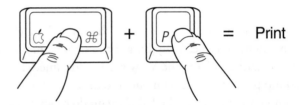

You don't have to bother learning the command-key equivalents if you don't want to use them. To make them easier to work into your routine, however, all Macintosh programs share a number of command-key equivalents for the most common operations (see table 5.1).

Table 5.1. Common Command-Key Equivalents

Key	Menu Command	What It Does
⌘-O	Open	Either opens a selected item directly or leads to a dialog that enables you to select something to open
⌘-N	New	Depends on program, but something new and blank (or untitled) will be created
⌘-P	Print	Begins the printing process

Key	Menu Command	What It Does
⌘-Q	Quit	Stops the current program
⌘-S	Save	Stores a copy of the current document to the hard disk
⌘-X	Cut	Deletes a selected item
⌘-C	Copy	Stores a copy of a selected item in memory
⌘-P	Paste	Inserts an item from memory
⌘-Z	Undo	Restores the state just prior to last action

A Menu's Menu

You probably will encounter in some programs an additional menu element: a right-facing triangle along the right edge of a menu. Newcomers find these *hierarchical menus* tricky, because they take a bit of careful mousing to access successfully. When you drag the pointer through a hierarchical menu item, a submenu appears to the right of the main menu (see fig. 5.12). To select an item in the submenu, the trick is to drag the pointer horizontally to the right until the pointer starts highlighting items. Then you can drag vertically within the submenu to make your selection (see fig. 5.13). If you let the pointer slide back into the main menu, the submenu disappears, and you have to do that tricky part again. Experienced Macintosh users swear by them or at them, but when hierarchical menus are built into a program, we all have to use them.

Figure 5.12
A menu item followed by a right-facing arrow means that a submenu will appear when selected.

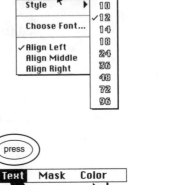

Figure 5.13
Choosing an item in a hierarchical menu takes some tricky mouse work.

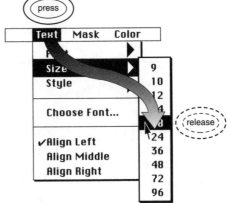

Menu Turn-Off

It may seem odd at first, but you must use the menus to turn off the Macintosh safely—even for those Macs that have the big switch on the back. In the Finder's Special menu is an item named Shut Down (see fig. 5.14). Choosing this item closes down all programs and makes sure that the hard disk is in order before turning the system off. In the case of Macintosh Classic, Performa 200 and 400, LC-style, and Centris machines, we still issue this command and then press the switch. (The dialog box shown in figure 5.15 tells us it's OK to do it.) There is no keyboard shortcut for shutting down except on the color Classic model.

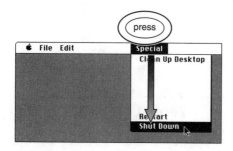

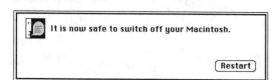

Figure 5.14
The Special menu contains the command that turns off most Macintoshes. Choose this item even if your Mac has a rear panel power switch.

Figure 5.15
Some Mac models display this message after you choose Shut Down. The Finder has cleaned up everything it needs to protect the hard disk and its contents.

Different from DOS

The consistency of having the same menus always available is simply not the case in DOS. In older DOS programs, you often have to "back your way out" of a particular part of a program to reach a menu of choices. Fortunately, due to early acceptance of standards recommended by Apple, software programmers have made it easy for users to know the program's basic commands even before tearing open the shrink wrap.

When a DOS program emulates the pull-down menu concept, the menus more likely stay pulled down until a choice is made or the menu is put away (pressing the Esc key, for instance). This feature is primarily to accommodate keyboard-only users who don't have the drag-type pointer control that mouse users have.

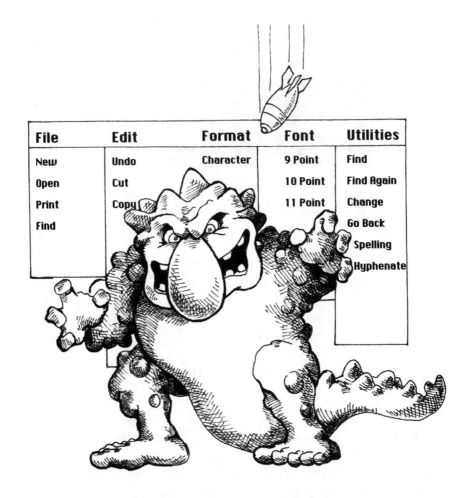

They're Out To Get Us

Sometimes a menu can be so long that its items can't fit in the vertical space of your screen. When that happens, the Macintosh comes to the rescue by turning the menu into a scrolling menu, indicated by the down-facing triangle at the bottom of the menu (see fig. 5.16). Drag below the menu in the direction of the arrow, and the menu scrolls (shifts) to reveal the other items; drag above the top of the menu to scroll back up. You can choose any undimmed item in the menu, even if it's not normally visible when you pull it down.

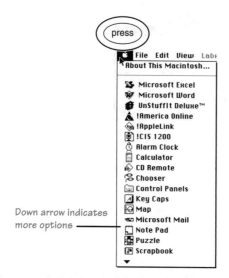

Down arrow indicates
more options ——

Figure 5.16
*When a menu is
longer than the
Desktop, a down
arrow indicates
that there are more
options. Drag below
the menu to let items
scroll into view.*

Depending on what else might be installed in your Macintosh, you may see
additional symbols in your menu bar (see fig. 5.17). Some of these items are
merely indicators, such as a PowerBook battery charge meter. Others are
menus that you can pull down. These items' meanings are tied directly to
the programs that put them there in the first place.

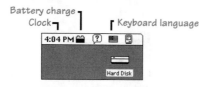

Figure 5.17
*Press and hold down
the pointer on an
unknown item to see
whether it is a menu.*

What happens if you make the wrong menu choice? It happens—regularly.
Fortunately, Macintosh program designers by and large have anticipated this
possibility. If you've made the wrong choice and something disastrous has
happened, you usually can take everything back by issuing the Undo command in the Edit menu shown in figure 5.18. (Although this command isn't
always available, it is in better programs). If the errant choice leads to a
dialog box, click the Cancel button, and all is put back the way it was.

Figure 5.18
Thank Heaven for Undo!

Practice

Mouse-Menu Action

1. Pull down the File menu.

2. Slowly drag down the File menu, watching closely how active items highlight as the pointer touches them and how dimmed items don't highlight (see fig. 5.19).

3. Notice dividers between groups of commands.

4. Drag the pointer to the right of the menu and release the mouse button to release the menu without making a selection.

Figure 5.19
As you drag down a menu, active items highlight, but dimmed (inactive) ones don't.

Check Out More Menus

1. Pull down the File menu but don't drag down the menu.

2. Keep pressing the mouse button down and drag the pointer to the Edit menu.

3. Notice the Undo, Cut, Copy, and Paste items, which virtually every program has.

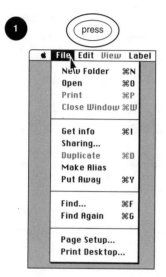

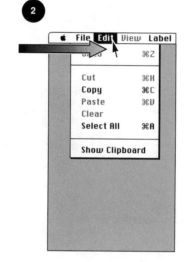

Figure 5.20
Hold the File menu open; then drag along the menu bar to pull down the next menu.

Make a Menu Choice

1. Pull down the Help menu.

2. Choose the About Balloon Help item (it has an ellipsis, so expect a dialog box to appear).

3. Watch closely as the chosen item flashes a few times before executing.

4. Click the OK button in the dialog box.

See How Menu Items Can Change

1. Pull down the Help menu and choose Show Balloons (see fig. 5.21). For now, try to ignore screen balloons that pop up.

Figure 5.21

Selecting Show Balloons... from the Help menu.

2. Pull down the Help menu again and notice that Show Balloons has changed to Hide Balloons, because the situation has changed (see fig. 5.22).

Figure 5.22

Menu item name has changed to the opposite—a common technique when a menu item switches a feature on and off.

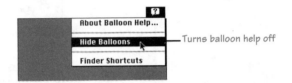

3. Choose Hide Balloons.

Changing from Dimmed to Active

1. Double-click the hard disk icon to open its window (in case it's not already open).

2. Click anywhere on the Desktop pattern (i.e., not in the window).

3. Pull down the File menu and notice that the Close Window item is dimmed, because no window is currently selected (see fig. 5.23).

4. Click anywhere in the Hard Disk window's white space. This action selects that window.

5. Pull down the File menu and see that Close Window is now active.

6. Choose Close Window from the File menu. This selection closes the window and selects the Hard Disk icon (it is highlighted).

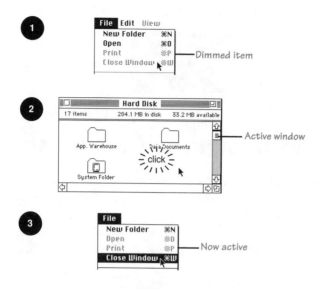

Figure 5.23
*Close Window
command is dimmed
(1) until you activate
a window by clicking
in it (2). Now you
can use the menu to
close the window (3).*

7. Click in the Desktop and look for the dimmed Open command in the
   File menu.

8. Click on the Hard Disk icon and now choose the active Open command in the File menu.

Command-Key Equivalents

1. Press Command-W (Close Window command) and watch the File
   menu name highlight briefly while the window closes.

2. Click in the Desktop and press Command-O (Open). Because the
   hard disk is not selected, there's nothing to open, and the Open
   command is inactive.

3. Click on the Hard Disk icon, as shown in figure 5.24, and press
   Command-O.

Figure 5.24
Select an item and press Command-O to operate the Open command from the keyboard.

Shutting Down the Macintosh

Choose Shut Down from the Special menu. If you see a dialog box that tells you it is safe to turn off your Macintosh, reach around to the power switch and turn off the machine.

Figure 5.25
Shut down your Macintosh at the end of this encounter.

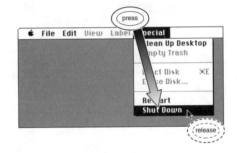

Summary

Menus are the primary way we tell the Macintosh what to do next. Even if we don't have a clue about what the next step may be in operating a program, pulling down the menus may jog our memories about what to do. Commands that all programs have in common are always in the same menu and go by the same name (or close enough); most of these commands can also be initiated by typing a keyboard equivalent—the Command key plus one other key. Finally, the safe way to shut off the Macintosh is through the Shut Down command in the Finder's Special menu.

Exorcises

1. An English-speaking student from Japan has brought her new Japanese (Kanji) language Macintosh to you for some help on how to use it. Match the following Desktop items to the callouts in the Kanji screen:

   a. menu bar

   b. Hard Disk icon

   c. Apple menu

   d. File menu

   e. Edit menu

   f. Help menu

   g. Application menu

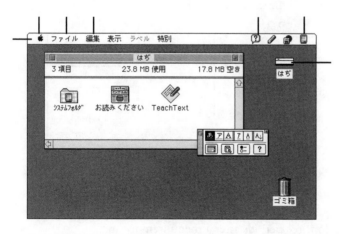

Figure 5.26
Japanese Desktop.

2. In the following Kanji Finder menus, locate these Macintosh commands by matching them to the callout lines in figure 5.27:

   a. Undo

   b. Cut

   c. Copy

d. Paste

e. About This Macintosh

f. Open

g. Close Window

h. Show or Hide Balloons

i. About Balloon Help

j. Shut Down

Figure 5.27
Japanese menus.

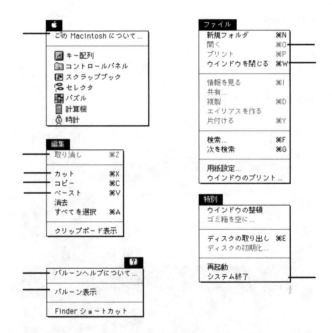

3. What do three periods after a menu item mean?

4. Match the following menu commands to their standard command-key equivalents:

____New	a. -C
____Open	b. -X
____Print	c. -Z
____Close Window	d. -O
____Quit	e. -V
____Undo	f. -P
____Cut	g. -N
____Copy	h. -W
____Paste	i. -Q

What's in Your Machine

Goal

Learn how to use the Finder to show you everything
you need to know about your Mac and its contents.

What You Will Need

Start with the Macintosh turned off.

Terms of Enfearment

System Folder	mounting
megabyte	folder
root	memory
volume	RAM
file server	kilobyte

Briefing

Earlier, I introduced the idea that the hard disk in your Macintosh is like a giant filing cabinet (see fig. 6.1). It contains documents, programs, and folders; those folders, in turn, can hold additional documents, programs, and other folders. The hard disk also contains a bunch of stuff that the Macintosh needs to behave like a Mac—it's all in a special folder called the *System Folder*.

Figure 6.1
Your hard disk is like a giant filing cabinet.

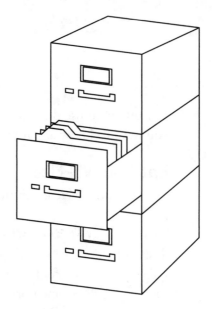

Half Full or Half Empty?

As you work with your Macintosh, you need to keep an eye on how much empty space there is in the hard disk so that you can store new documents. Hard disks are measured in a unit called the *megabyte* (one megabyte is equivalent to approximately one million typed characters). The Finder can tell you at a glance how many megabytes of your hard disk are occupied and how many are available for additional stuff. Opening the hard disk window and viewing the contents by icon (as controlled by the View menu), the Finder displays this information and keeps it up to date as items are added or deleted (see fig. 6.2).

Figure 6.2
Every Finder window can show how much space is available, such as this example of a 120-megabyte disk drive.

Also at the top of the window is the number of items in the current window, even if you can't see all of them (see fig. 6.3). This number can be deceiving until you become familiar with your Mac, because it counts a folder as one item, even if there are hundreds of items inside it.

Figure 6.3
Every Finder window also shows the number of items in the window.

Desktop Icons

What you see in the hard disk's own window (the one that opens when you double-click the Hard Disk icon) is said to be at the *root* level. You won't hear the term too much, but you should be aware of it just in case. Each Hard Disk icon you see on the Desktop is also known by another generic name—a *volume* (see fig. 6.4). The hard disk is a volume; if the disk is divided (partitioned) into multiple segments, each segment is called a volume, because it has its own icon. Opening up any volume shows you how much space is taken up and available just for that volume. If an external hard disk is also connected to your Mac, its icon appears on the screen (usually below the internal startup volume) and is also called a volume. Macintoshes in a corporate environment may also be connected to disks on other computers. One of those disks, represented by an icon (with the funny cables running to and from it) is also a volume, as well as being called a *file server* (a hard disk that *serves up* files for other computers to use).

Figure 6.4
Desktops can get crowded with many volumes, including multiple disk drives and network file servers.

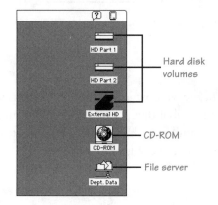

If you don't want an extraneous volume appearing on the Desktop, you can make it unavailable by dragging it to the Trash (see fig. 6.5). No, this doesn't erase the disk (although you might think so from the name of the action); it just removes it from the Desktop. To make the volume reappear on the Desktop, you need to restart the Macintosh (a choice in the Finder's Special menu) or use a software program designed to put a volume on the Desktop (called *mounting* a volume).

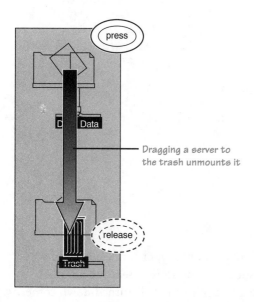

Dragging a server to
the trash unmounts it

Figure 6.5
*It may seem weird,
but dragging a file
server volume to the
Trash removes it
from your Desktop—
nothing is lost or
erased on the server.*

Filing Cabinet Folders

In the hard disk window, you probably see one or more *folder* icons. Just like the paper folders of the old-fashioned office (like the offices we all work in), folders enable us to collect related stuff, label the folder by name, and carry everything in the folder as one convenient item. Macintosh folders, however, aren't limited in how many things they can hold. In fact, they can even hold other folders, which can hold other folders, and so on, until you probably have lost what it is you were trying to organize.

One folder is so special, the Macintosh even knows to show a special icon for it: the *System Folder* (see fig. 6.6). You don't have to do too much in the System Folder, but your Macintosh can't operate without a number of the elements in there. Later, we'll have a peek inside and see some of the specifics. Fortunately, the Mac lets us drag-and-drop relevant items to the System Folder where the Finder takes over to place them in more nested folders as needed.

Figure 6.6

A Macintosh folder may contain thousands of items or nothing. One special folder, the System Folder, must be on every Macintosh. Its icon is different from all other folder icons.

Other Icons

Finder windows can have all kinds of plain, pretty, or confusing icons in them (see fig. 6.7). The most artistic ones tend to represent programs. Document icons vary a lot but usually display a telltale turned-down corner. I'll have more to say about these items later.

Figure 6.7

Some application icons (top) and their related document icons (bottom). Usually, there is a family resemblance between an application and its document icons.

FileMaker Pro

Microsoft Excel

Information Manager

FileMaker Database

Excel Spreadsheet

CompuServe E-Mail

Short-Term Memory

The other critical measurement of your Mac's capabilities is something called *memory* (also, interchangeably, *RAM* for random access memory). Memory is measured in terms of *kilobytes*, or thousands of characters, represented by the letter K, and *megabytes* (M, MB, or Megs).

When discussing the amount of RAM inside a Macintosh, the megabyte number is the one to use. The value is generally a number ranging from two to tens of megabytes (see fig. 6.8). The maximum amount of RAM the Macintosh may hold depends entirely on the model of Macintosh you have; the minimum recommended for productive work is four megabytes.

Figure 6.8
Memory is expandable to different amounts, depending on the Macintosh model.

Memory Check

To check how much RAM is installed in your Macintosh, choose About This Macintosh from the Apple Menu. The dialog box shown in figure 6.9 appears and shows a number of important items about your Mac: the Macintosh model, System software version, total memory, and many more items that aren't important right now. The total memory value is related in kilobytes (K). To correlate this value to a megabyte rating, divide the K number by 1,024 (I don't have the time to explain, and you probably don't have the patience to learn, how a computer considers a thousand of anything to actually be 1,024). For example, a total memory of 8,192K evaluates to 8 megabytes (see fig. 6.10).

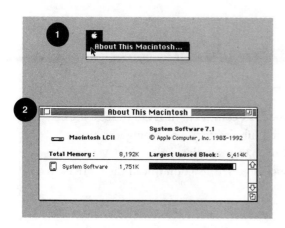

Figure 6.9
Choosing About This Macintosh from the Apple menu leads you to an informative window.

Figure 6.10

To translate a kilobyte measurement to a megabyte measurement, divide by 1,024.

$$8192K \div 1024 = 8M$$

Two Different Animals

RAM is very different from disk storage. RAM is temporary. The instant you shut down your Mac, contents of RAM are forgotten history (see fig. 6.11). RAM is like a chalkboard in a classroom. To work on a problem for the class, the teacher copies a problem from the lesson plan onto the board. While working on the problem, all action is on the blackboard. Because the board will be washed clean at night, it is vital that the work in progress be copied down on paper and stored away (in a filing cabinet) so that it can be retrieved tomorrow. That's why our machines have hard disks that act like filing cabinets: to preserve great amounts of information from session to session.

Figure 6.11

When you turn off your Mac, the contents of RAM are erased.

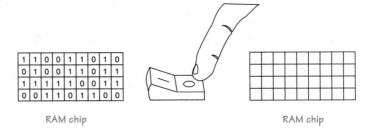

RAM chip   RAM chip

Different from DOS

Unlike constantly typing the DIR command in DOS to see a list of items in the currently selected subdirectory—or typing a tortuous backslash-laden command to change subdirectories—the Macintosh lets us view a directory at a glance. We also don't need the CHKDSK command to check hard disk and memory space. We can even switch instantly from any program to the Finder to find out the condition of our hard disk space. On the Macintosh, folders replace the concept of subdirectories. Moreover, names of folders can be up to 32 characters, instead of the eight character limit of DOS.

On the RAM side, you may have encountered the difficulties in managing large amounts of DOS memory (the terms *expanded* and *extended* memory may ring bells). On the Macintosh, RAM is one contiguous workspace, which can grow or shrink depending on how many memory chips are installed in the machine at any moment.

They're Out To Get Us

If you look at the numbers of hard disk space used and available, you may discover that the total doesn't seem to add up to what you thought the hard disk's capacity was (see fig. 6.12). Hard disk sizes are approximate, and some of a disk's available space is used privately by the computer, so it doesn't show up as part of the total of items occupying the space.

Figure 6.12
Hard disk sizes are approximate.

44.3 MB in disk + 74.4 MB available = 120 MB??

Sometimes a hard disk can fill up. When this happens, you could be in trouble if you need to save changes to a big document. There are ways to get out of the jam, but the best solution is to avoid getting too full in the first place. I make some recommendations about this situation in the 21st Encounter.

Figure 6.13
A 40M hard disk that is running out of disk space. Anything under 1 megabyte is getting tight.

One gotcha on the RAM side is that it's not as easy to install additional RAM as everyone would like you to believe. Not only do you have to open the case (which requires special tools for the PowerBook and Classic), but you often have to remove a number of components to get to the sockets for RAM modules.

Practice

Check the Hard Disk

1. Start your Macintosh as you learned in the 2nd Encounter.

2. From the Desktop, double-click the hard disk icon to open its window (see fig. 6.14).

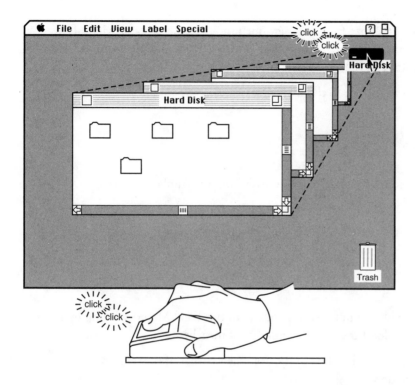

Figure 6.14
Double-clicking on the Hard Disk icon opens its window.

3. Choose Icon from the View menu. Notice how in this menu the Macintosh marks the current setting with a checkmark in the list of possible views (see fig. 6.15).

Figure 6.15
Set the view of the window to by Icon.

4. Add up the number in the "in disk" and "available" listings to find the approximate capacity of your hard disk. What do you think your hard disk is rated at from the factory?

5. Choose Size from the View menu to get an at-a-glance view of the items in your root directory. Notice the size of items rated in kilobytes (K).

6. Change back to the Icon view.

Check the RAM

1. Choose About This Macintosh from the Apple Menu (see fig. 6.16).

Figure 6.16
Choose About This Macintosh from the Apple menu.

2. Divide the number of kilobytes in the Total Memory listing by 1024. Say aloud the resulting number of megabytes.

3. Click the close box in the upper left corner of the window to hide the window.

Figure 6.17
Click the small box in the window's upper left corner to close the window.

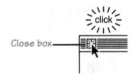

Summary

The hard disk is the long-term storage area for documents and programs. Items can be organized into folders, which may be nested inside other folders. Disk space is measured in megabytes (MB), but items on the disk are usually measured in kilobytes (K). It takes 1,024 kilobytes to make one megabyte. RAM is a temporary storage area where actual work is done on documents by programs. RAM contents are erased when the machine shuts down, so all work is saved to the hard disk.

Exorcises

1. If you write and store 10 business letters a day, and each letter occupies 4K (roughly 4,000 characters) of disk space, how many days will it take you to fill up one megabyte of disk space?

2. Classify the icons in table 6.1 as being volumes, documents, programs, or folders by filling in the third column.

Table 6.1. Classify the Icons

Icon	Name	Classification
	standard folder	_____
	standard application	_____
	standard document	_____
	Word document	_____
	Excel	_____
	shared folder	_____
	hard disk	_____
	file server	_____
	FileMaker data file	_____

3. How many megabytes of RAM are in the Macintosh whose About
   This Macintosh window is shown in figure 6.18?

Figure 6.18
*About This Macin-
tosh window.*

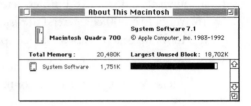

4. In the Application menu shown in figure 6.19, name the applications
   currently running on this Macintosh.

Figure 6.19
Application menu.

5. Why is the Show All item in the Application menu dimmed?

Window
with a View

Goal

Learn how the Finder displays the contents of folders in on-screen windows and how to manage windows most efficiently.

What You Will Need

Macintosh turned on, showing the Desktop.

Terms of Enfearment

title bar	zoom box
active window	close box
grow box	scroll bar

Briefing

We've seen some windows previously, but now it's time to examine Finder windows more closely (see fig. 7.1). The Macintosh likes to give us lots of flexibility in the way we do things on the screen, and Finder windows are no exception. Even better, what we learn about Finder windows applies to most other windows in Macintosh work.

Figure 7.1
Finder windows hold icons for folders, files, and applications.

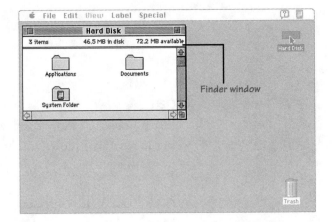

Entitlebarment

Windows contain several controls that let us determine how things look and where they are. For instance, across the top of every Finder window is the *title bar* (see fig. 7.2). The name in the title bar is the name of the volume or folder we've opened. Horizontal black stripes stretching across the title bar also tell a story: the window showing those stripes is called the *active window* (see fig. 7.3). This is the window—among however many layers of windows

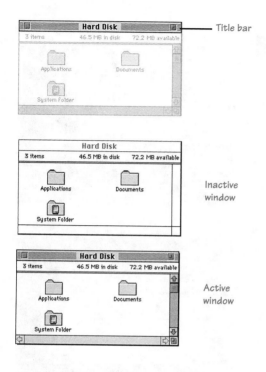

Title bar

Figure 7.2
Windows title bar.

Inactive
window

Active
window

Figure 7.3
*Inactive window
and active window.
Stripes appear in the
title bar of only the
active window on
the Desktop.*

that may be on the screen—that is on top of the pile, just like the item that's on top of the heap of stuff strewn around your physical desk. Only one Finder window can be active at a time. An inactive window lacks these stripes. To switch among active windows, all it takes is a click of the pointer anywhere on the window, even if only on the slightest sliver hanging out from beneath another window on the screen.

The title bar is also the means by which we move windows around the screen. Click and drag in the title bar. As we drag the window, we drag just its outline (see fig. 7.4). Position the outline where we want it, release the mouse button, and the actual window zips to that spot.

Figure 7.4
To move a window,
drag its title bar.

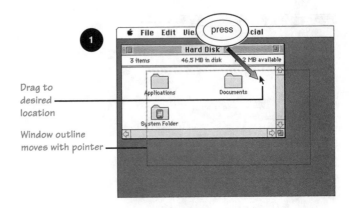

Drag to
desired
location

Window outline
moves with pointer

Resizing Windows

We can also resize a window. By clicking and dragging the *grow box* at the lower right corner of the window, the window can be adjusted to any size or proportion we like. As we drag the grow box, we see the outline of the window change in size (see fig. 7.5). Only the lower right corner is adjustable. To size and position a window in a new corner of the screen, for instance, requires resizing and moving the window.

While we're on the subject of resizing a window, notice the little box at the right edge of the title bar. This is called a *zoom box.* When we click it in the Finder, the window automatically sizes itself—within the confines of the screen size—to show as much of the window's contents as possible and no more (see fig. 7.6). Another click of the zoom box restores the size to where it was before.

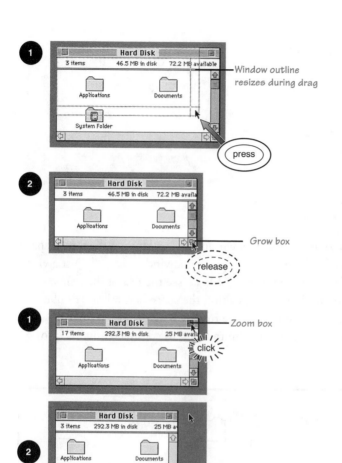

Window outline
resizes during drag

press

Figure 7.5
To resize a window, drag the grow box in the lower right corner.

Grow box

release

Zoom box

click

Figure 7.6
A click of the zoom box sizes the window to the best fit for items in the window. Click again to restore the previous size.

Window at
optimum size

Closing Windows

At the left edge of the title bar is a speedcut button for closing the window (the clunky way is to use the Close Window menu command). When we click this *close box*, we see the window zip back to the volume or folder icon whence it came (see fig. 7.7). By now, we already know the speedcut for opening a window—double-clicking on a volume or folder window.

Figure 7.7
*Clicking the close
box closes the
window.*

A Vast Vista

Quite often, the amount of stuff in a window is greater than the screen space
available for it. Here's where we get to see that a window is really just a view
to what may be a larger space (see fig. 7.8). To see the rest of the items, we
don't reposition the window, we reposition the space beneath it. It's like
working with a microfilm or microfiche reader: we view the contents
through a fixed lens and move the film to bring the desired contents into
view.

Figure 7.8
*A window is just a
view to a larger
space.*

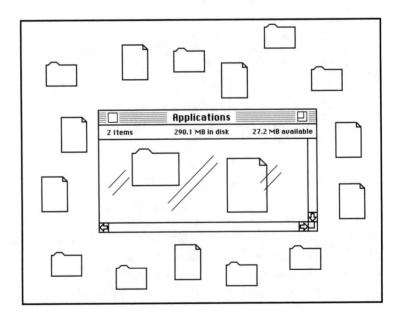

Our controls for moving the window's contents are called *scroll bars*. Space for scroll bars is reserved along the right and bottom edges of Finder windows (and lots of other Mac windows, too). When everything in the folder is visible in the window, the scroll bar areas are blank. Only when there's more stuff outside of our view does one or both scroll bars come to life (see fig. 7.9).

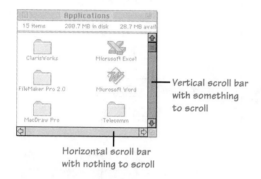

Vertical scroll bar with something to scroll

Horizontal scroll bar with nothing to scroll

Figure 7.9
Scroll bars let us adjust our view to a larger space than shows through the window.

Scroll Bar Pieces

A live scroll bar has five elements to help navigate in either the vertical or horizontal direction (see fig. 7.10). At each edge of a scroll bar are arrow buttons. A click of the button scrolls the window's view of the contents in that direction by one unit (this unit varies with the type of information being viewed in the window). Note the distinction—we scroll in the direction of our view to the contents, not the direction that the contents move.

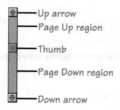

Up arrow
Page Up region
Thumb
Page Down region
Down arrow

Figure 7.10
An active scroll bar consists of five controls we click or drag (thumb) to adjust our view.

As we scroll in any direction, an indicator shows the position of the current view in relation to the available space—the gray pattern area of the scroll bar (see fig. 7.11). It's like an electronic version of knowing how far we are in a book, where we can see the bulk of pages we've passed compared to the chunk yet to go. Clicking and holding down on a scroll bar arrow puts scrolling in rapid-fire action.

Figure 7.11
The position of the thumb shows our current view relative to the entire scrollable space in that direction.

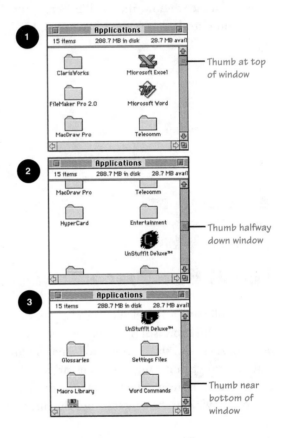

Thumb at top of window

Thumb halfway down window

Thumb near bottom of window

To jump to some approximate spot, we can click and drag this indicator (called the *thumb*, but hardly any users know this) to about where we want to go and then fine tune the view with the arrow buttons. Unfortunately, the view doesn't change as we drag the thumb. We must release the mouse button to see where we are (see fig. 7.12). (Some programs do, however, provide indicators to help out.)

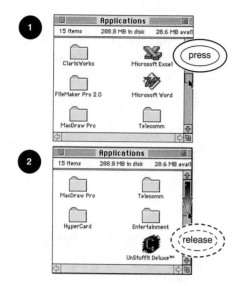

Figure 7.12
We can drag the thumb to any spot along the scroll bar to jump ahead or back. The view doesn't change until we release the mouse button.

One other scrolling increment at our disposal—clicking in the gray area on either side of the thumb—shifts our view in windowful chunks. These clickable areas are called Page Up and Page Down controls, which helps explain their function, but these aren't critical terms to remember. What is important is knowing how they shift the view so that we can quickly maneuver our way through a chock-full window.

Change of View

The Finder provides a number of ways of viewing a window's contents. The primary choices are between icons and text listings, with further variations of each. Each window remembers what type of view it has—closing and reopening the window doesn't affect the view type. We can also mix view types among various windows on the Desktop.

Changing a window's view is as simple as clicking in the window to activate it (the horizontal stripes come alive) and choosing a view type from the

Finder's View menu (see fig. 7.13). Usually, the best view for beginners is the standard Icon view, because the icons are easy to distinguish and click on; there probably isn't too much stuff on the hard disk yet. The Small Icon view allows for more items to be visible within a given window space (see fig. 7.14).

Figure 7.13

We can change how the Finder displays a window's contents via the View menu.

Figure 7.14

The small icon view shows more items per square inch, while giving us flexibility in the layout of items.

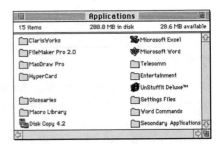

Text views are all the same except for the manner in which items in the window are sorted: alphabetically by name or other attributes; numerically by size; or chronologically by the date of an item's last modification. For windows with lots of items in them, text views can be quite efficient, because they not only show more items per square inch of window space, but by having items sorted in lists, a desired item may be easier to locate (see fig. 7.15).

Figure 7.15

Text views are compact but more rigid. The under-lined column heading shows how the window is sorted. Click on a column heading as a speed cut to sorting by other attributes.

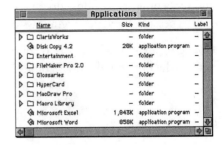

Text Outline View

Conveniently, text views act like electronic outlines if we wish. Yes, there's still a subminiature icon next to each item indicating document, program, or folder, but we don't have to open up another window to view the contents of a folder. A right facing triangle next to a folder is a control that lets us expand the view of the folder right within the same list view. Any item we can see, we can drag to another folder, volume, or Desktop, just as its iconic equivalent. We can keep opening these text outlines as deeply as there are folders nested within others (see fig. 7.16). The more stuff that accumulates in a folder, the more likely you'll switch to a text view of one type or another.

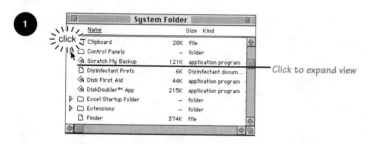

Click to expand view

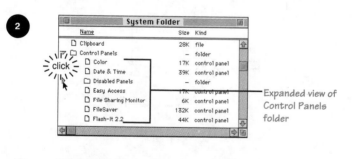

Expanded view of Control Panels folder

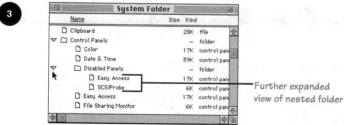

Further expanded view of nested folder

Figure 7.16
Text views can be expanded in an outline structure. We can see the contents of nested folders all in one window.

Different from DOS

Except for Microsoft Windows, there is no standard for the appearance and behavior of windows or their controls in programs. And DOS doesn't provide the flexibility of working with files or subdirectories as distinct windows.

They're Out To Get Us

Because it is easy to activate an underlying window by clicking on it, the strong possibility exists that a newly activated window will completely obscure a smaller window that had previously been on top. The small window isn't gone. In fact, unless you specifically close it, the window will always be there. To access this obscured window in the Finder, you'll have to move and/or resize other windows until you can see any part of the smaller window to click on and make it the active window again (see fig. 7.17).

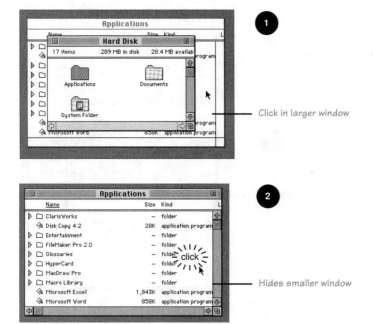

Click in larger window

Figure 7.17
A click on a larger, underlying window can completely hide the smaller window. It takes some window maneuvering to view the smaller one.

Hides smaller window

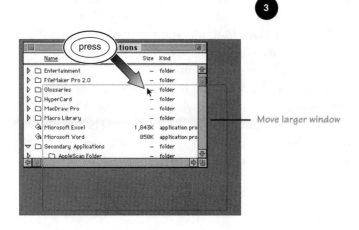

Move larger window

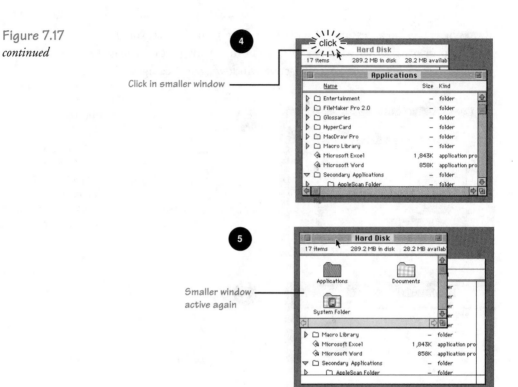

Figure 7.17
continued

Click in smaller window

Smaller window
active again

As you work with the Mac, you may encounter a number of other window styles, some of which are standard Macintosh material, and others that were designed by programmers to mimic window styles from other computer systems (see fig. 7.18). On the Macintosh side, you may find window styles that lack one or more of the following: scroll bars, grow box, zoom box, or close box. Moreover, the title bar may look quite different. When a control is missing, it usually means that the window's behavior is narrower than, say, Finder windows. This is perfectly legal. But, when you encounter a truly strange window, you'll have to figure out how the weird scroll bars work or what, if any, other controls exist. Most products that try to re-design the traditional Macintosh window styles change back after protests from customers.

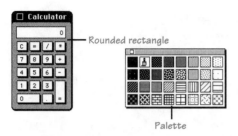

Rounded rectangle

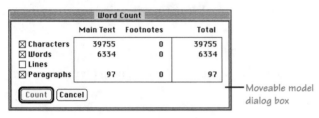

Palette

Figure 7.18
A few of the many window styles used in Macintosh programs. They all have recognizable elements.

Word Count	Main Text	Footnotes	Total
☒ Characters	39755	0	39755
☒ Words	6334	0	6334
☐ Lines			
☒ Paragraphs	97	0	97

[Count] [Cancel]

Moveable model dialog box

Practice

Window Calisthenics

1. Open the Hard Disk window.

2. Drag the window around the screen by its title bar; release the mouse button. Do this several times to get the feel of dragging the window outline. Leave the window in a position so that the grow box (lower right corner) is visible.

3. Drag the grow box and resize the window a couple of times. See how small you can resize the window. Then resize the window to an intermediate size.

4. Click the zoom box (upper right corner) to see how the Finder sizes the window to its optimum size (within the limits of your screen). Click the zoom box again to restore the window to its previous size.

5. If you can't see the System Folder in your hard disk window, type the letters "sy" quickly. This should locate the System Folder (see fig. 7.19). (Hey! What a great speedcut to find something in the active window!) Open the folder.

Figure 7.19
The System Folder.

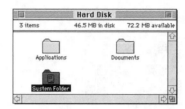

6. Click the zoom box to bring the System Folder window to optimum size.

7. Choose each view from the View menu and notice the differences between views. Choose the Name view before going on to the next step (see fig. 7.20).

Figure 7.20
*Choose each view
and watch the
window contents.*

Text View Convenience

1. Double-click the Apple Menu Items Folder to open its window (see fig. 7.21).

Figure 7.21
*The Apple Menu
Items window*

2. Close the window.

3. As an alternate way to see the contents of that folder, click on the triangle next to the Apple Menu Items Folder entry to reveal the next level of items in that folder in the text listing (see fig. 7.22).

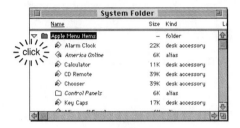

Figure 7.22
Text view of Apple Menu Items from the System Folder window.

4. Click the triangle again to cinch up the listing.

Scrolling

1. Resize the System Folder menu to the size shown in figure 7.23.

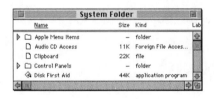

Figure 7.23
Resize System Folder window.

2. Click the down arrow several times to scroll line-by-line.

3. Note the last item in the window and click the page down region of the vertical scroll bar. Note the first item now in the window.

4. Drag the thumb to the very bottom of the scroll bar and release the mouse button. Then drag it to the top and release.

5. Choose Icon view and repeat steps 2 through 4 to see how scrolling, paging, and thumbing feels in an iconic view.

6. Click on any icon in the System Folder; then choose Name in the View menu (see fig. 7.24). Notice how the selected item is still selected, even though the window looks entirely different.

Figure 7.24
Select an item in one view, and it remains selected in a different view, although you may have to scroll the window to see the item.

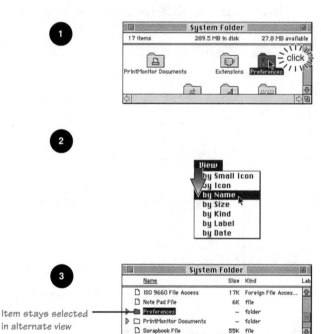

Close 'em All Speedcut

1. Double-click a few folders to show three or more windows.

2. Hold down the Option key and click the close box of the active window (see fig. 7.25). Notice how all windows (including the hard disk volume) close up. How's that for cleaning your Desktop in a hurry?

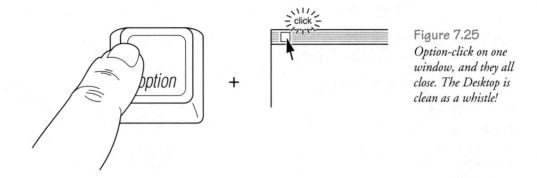

Figure 7.25
Option-click on one window, and they all close. The Desktop is clean as a whistle!

Summary

We've learned much more about how windows let us see items contained on the hard disk and the various ways we can view those items. No matter how many windows are open on the Desktop, only one—the active window—is on top of the pile. Window controls found in Finder windows—for moving, resizing, zooming, scrolling, and closing—are the same controls you'll find in other windows throughout your Macintosh work.

Exorcises

1. Match the window components' names to the blanks on the illustration in figure 7.26.

    a. title bar

    b. close box

    c. zoom box

d. grow box

e. horizontal scroll bar

f. vertical scroll bar

g. window name

Figure 7.26
*Fill-in the blank
with the letter of the
corresponding term
from exorcise 1.*

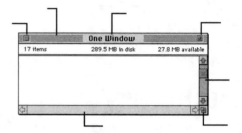

2. Describe what happens when you click on or drag the following window controls:

a. grow box

b. scroll down arrow

c. page down area

d. title bar

3. Name three ways to close a Finder window.

8th Encounter

Getting Organized

Goal

To set up a practical Desktop window layout and hard disk folder organization with which to start your Macintosh work.

What You Will Need

Macintosh turned on, showing the Desktop.

Terms of Enfearment

application
document
file
Get Info dialog box
autoscrolling
overlapping windows
tiled windows

Briefing

Folders Full of Files

As we'll see later, the work we really do with the Macintosh is inside *application* programs—things like word processors, spreadsheets, databases, and the like. All of these programs generate *documents*, which we store on the hard disk (see fig. 8.1). Each document, as well as each program, resides on the hard disk as a *file*. This is an old computing term that dates back to before many of us were born.

Figure 8.1
Application file icons (top row) and their corresponding document file icons (bottom row). Often, there is a resemblance.

Real-World versus Computer Files

In a filing cabinet metaphor, our idea of a file may be confused by the typical practice to casually refer to a file as a folder of stuff. If you were ever hauled down to the principal's office, your file (a folder from the filing cabinet) would have been front-and-center on the principal's desk. In computerdom, however, each separate document in that folder (your attendance record, your grades, the forged absentee excuse) is considered a file (see fig. 8.2).

Figure 8.2
A Macintosh folder can hold any number of files or other folders.

Essentially, a file is a separate entity on the hard disk that has a name and many other attributes that differentiate it from other files. A program like Microsoft Word, for example, is a file unto itself, but it also relies on other files that give the program powers to check the spelling of our documents, to remember program settings we've made, and to perform automatic hyphenation. Each document (e.g., letter, memo, newsletter article) we create and name is also a separate file that resides on the hard disk.

The bottom line? Any icon we see on the Desktop—except folders, disk volumes, and the Trash—is a file. Period.

Tell Us More

Although text views of our Finder windows highlight a file's Finder attributes (e.g., name, approximate size, kind of file, date it was last modified), it's possible to see even more. To view these details, we can select the item and choose Get Info from the File menu. Although there's probably more there than we care to know, the *Get Info dialog* does tell us if a file is an application, a document (from a particular application), or a folder (see fig. 8.3). We also see its exact size, its location on our hard disk, and other data. We don't, however, see anything about the file's contents—we need the application for that.

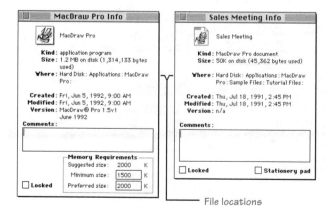

File locations

Figure 8.3
*Get Info dialog boxes
for an application
and a document file
it created.*

Why Organize?

Organizing these files on your hard disk is an important maintenance task. It's like checking the oil periodically on your car: you can ignore it for a while, but if you let it go forever, you're likely to get into trouble of some kind.

Because your hard disk may eventually contain thousands of files, it is important to establish a method to the madness. How you organize the files depends a lot on your view of your computing world. Two of the most common ways of grouping items are by application and by subject.

One (Old-Fashioned) Method

Organizing a hard disk by application is more computer oriented. Such an organization is shown in figure 8.4. At the root level are folders for each application. The implication is that documents for each application are stored inside those folders as well (perhaps inside other folders).

Figure 8.4
Organization by application makes us think too much in computer terms ("what program created that document I need?").

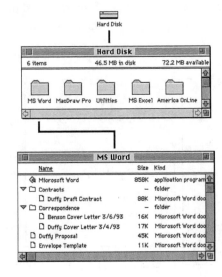

One (Recommended) Method

Organizing the disk by subject is more like the way you organize a filing cabinet and is the method I recommend. Figure 8.5 shows a typical way to start such an organization at the root level. It groups all application programs into one folder, called Applications. Thus, you know that if you want to start a program of any kind, you can open this folder (we'll also learn speedcuts later that let us bypass opening that folder).

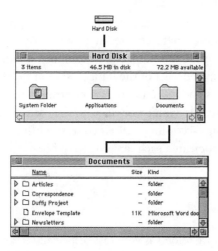

Figure 8.5
Organizing files by subject is more like a filing cabinet.

Another folder, called Documents, is where you will store all files that you create. Inside will be additional folders, named for their subject—along the same lines as you would categorize, group, and file them in a filing cabinet (see fig. 8.6). Examples would be folders for all correspondence for a given month; a folder for a project; a folder for a customer; a folder for all financial information.

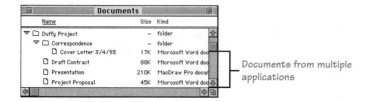

Documents from multiple applications

Figure 8.6
We can easily combine documents from different applications in a subject folder. Here, we have all the relevant files for the Duffy project in one folder.

> **Performa owners note:** You should use the Documents folder that first appeared on the Desktop as the Documents folder we speak about here. It has a special folder icon that features a small document icon.

Why the By-Subject Method Is Better

The reason this method makes more sense than the by-application method is that we are now free to use whatever combination of programs we want to generate documents for the given subject. For example, a folder for a specific project may contain a spreadsheet of the budget, several word processing documents for proposals and correspondence, electronic mail messages between the participants, electronic drawings, project schedules, and so on. You think of these things according to their context within your work life, not by the program that created each document.

New Folders

Using the Finder to create folders is very easy, especially in an icon view window (see fig. 8.7). Activate the window where you would like a new folder and choose New Folder (Command-N) from the File menu. A new, untitled folder appears, ready for us to type a name for it. Folder names can be up to 31 characters long—the only restriction being that we cannot use a colon symbol (see fig. 8.8). Anything else goes, including bullets and foreign language letters.

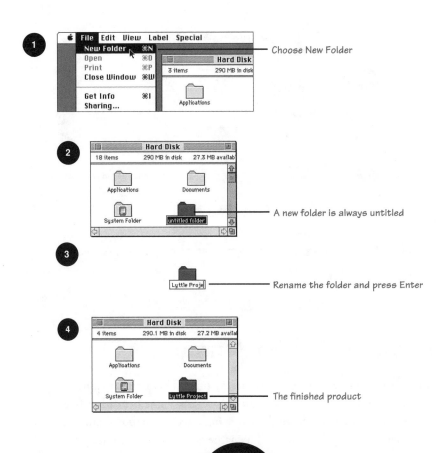

1 Choose New Folder

2 A new folder is always untitled

3 Rename the folder and press Enter

4 The finished product

Figure 8.7
Creating a folder in the Icon view. It first appears as an untitled folder, with its name read to be replaced by the next keys we type. Then press Enter to make the new name official.

Figure 8.8
Don't use the colon symbol when naming a folder.

In a text view, the Finder creates the folder at the level of the active window, no matter what other subfolders we have expanded or selected in the view (see fig. 8.9). The Finder also places the untitled folder in the appropriate place in the list, depending on how we've selected the sorting order in the View menu.

Figure 8.9
*Adding a new folder
in a text view works
the same way, except
it gets sorted the
instant we lock in
the folder name.*

Figure 8.9
*Adding a new folder
in a text view works
the same way, except
it gets sorted the
instant we lock in
the folder name.*

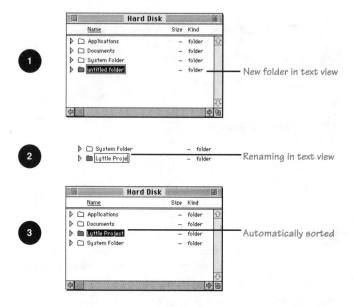

New folder in text view

Renaming in text view

Automatically sorted

Changing a Folder Name

After a folder is named, we can rename it at any time. This action requires clicking not just on the folder icon, but directly on the name beneath it (see fig. 8.10). After a brief pause, the folder name has a rectangle drawn around it, meaning that it is ready for editing. The name is automatically selected, so we can just type to replace the existing name with the new name. To lock in the new name, press the Return or Enter keys or click anywhere other than on the icon. This technique for renaming folders also applies to renaming files and even volumes on the Desktop.

Figure 8.10
*To select an item's
name for editing,
click on the name,
not the icon.*

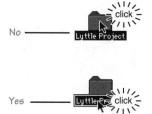

Moving Items Around

Moving a file or folder from one location to another is as simple as dragging the item to the desired location and dropping it either in a window or atop a folder (see fig. 8.11). Item moving is available in all window views, but for newcomers, the icon views seem to be easier to master. The only thing to remember is that for the smoothest ride, you should be able to see *both* the item you want moved and its destination.

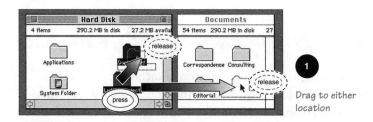

 Drag to either location

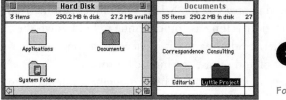 Folder is moved

Figure 8.11
To move an item into another folder, drag it to the folder icon or the folder's open window. The results are the same.

Dragging an item to a text view can be tricky if the window contains folders or if some nested folder levels are open. As you drag an item into the window, exercise care in where you drop it (see fig. 8.12). If the intended destination is merely inside the window, then be sure no other folder in the window highlights before you release the mouse button; when a folder is highlighted, the item goes into that folder instead. To drag an item into a nested folder, don't release it where the other items are listed: release it atop the highlighted folder.

Figure 8.12
*Moving an item into
a text view window
requires care. If a
folder highlights in
the destination
window, it means
that the dragged
item will go inside
the highlighted
folder.*

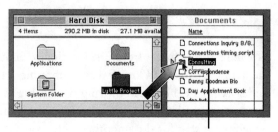

Make sure destination highlights

When the Window's Too Small

Although text views keep items sorted in the order dictated by the View
menu, no such restriction applies to either of the icon views. To reposition
an item in the window, drag it to the destination. If that destination is
beyond the visible area of the window, drag and hold down the item just
beyond the edge of the viewing area (see fig. 8.13). The Finder automatically
scrolls the view in that direction as long as you continue to hold down the
mouse button. When the desired destination is in view, then continue
dragging the item to that spot and release the mouse button. This
autoscrolling takes some getting used to, but it beats dragging an item out to
the Desktop, manually scrolling the window, and then dragging the item
back into the window—a perfectly legal maneuver in either case.

Smart Windows

Remember, too, that windows remember their sizes and locations when
they're closed. So, you can lay out key windows in advance and have them
open in a way that makes sense to you. For example, you can have windows
overlap or have them *tile* (laid out puzzle-piece style)—or combinations
thereof. Figure 8.14 shows one example layout that employs a combination
of overlapping and tiled windows.

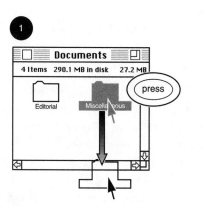

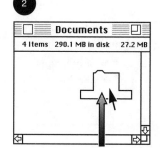

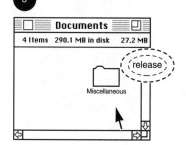

Figure 8.13
Dragging an item beyond the edge of the active area automatically scrolls the window in that direction.

Figure 8.14
A combination of tiled and overlapping windows in an effective Desktop layout.

Tiled windows

Overlapping windows

Different from DOS

Most DOS and Windows applications automatically install themselves inside an application-specific subdirectory. This appears to be in anticipation of the user storing related documents in that same subdirectory. It certainly makes opening and storing documents easier in DOS, because you don't then have to type the long pathnames to other subdirectories. The Macintosh, on the other hand, encourages you to organize files the way that makes the most sense to you, not the computer.

The whole concept of subdirectories—creating them, moving files from one to another, and deleting them—is vastly simplified by the Macintosh folder concept. Although the Macintosh internally keeps track of full pathnames, you never have to see them or remember commands to deal with them.

They're Out To Get Us

To help itself keep things straight, the Macintosh (or any personal computer for that matter) doesn't allow two items to have the same name at the same folder level. A hard disk may contain 20 files and folders named "Joe Blow," but no more than one can be at the same folder level (or on the Desktop). If you try to drag an item to a folder containing another item by the same name, the Finder alerts you to the fact and puts things back the way they were before you dragged (see fig. 8.15).

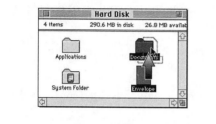

Figure 8.15
The Mac warns us when we're about to copy a file to a folder that already contains a file of that name.

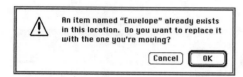

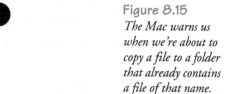

You don't have to be a neatness freak to realize that a junked up Desktop can get unruly in a hurry. Try to keep it clean. Also, it will be helpful if you keep the root level relatively clutter-free. It's OK to bring a folder you're using a lot to the Desktop or root but put it back when access requirements diminish.

Some Macintosh experts follow self-imposed guidelines about how many items should be at any given level. You can develop your own scheme as you get used to the system: you are in charge. We'll learn in the next encounter how to search a hard disk for anything in case you forget where a file is.

If there is one teeth-gritting frustration in working with files and folders, it's having things happen—creating a new folder and moving a file into a folder—in the wrong folder level. This is apt to happen more in text views than icon views. Fortunately, nothing we do (short of emptying the Trash in the 9th Encounter) is irreparable, so we can keep dragging things around until they're where we want them.

Practice

Creating and Naming Folders

1. Activate the hard disk window by clicking in the window or double-clicking the hard disk icon.

2. Choose New Folder from the File menu. Note the name, "untitled folder."

3. Choose New Folder again. Note the name, which is different from the other untitled folder (see fig. 8.16).

Figure 8.16
A second untitled folder appears in the window.

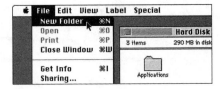

4. Click on the first *untitled folder*. You cannot edit its name yet.

5. Click on the name *below* the folder icon. The name highlights, and an edit box appears around it.

6. Type *My New Folder* and press Return to replace the original name (see fig. 8.17).

Figure 8.17
*Naming My New
Folder.*

7. Rename untitled folder 2 to *My New Folder.* Notice the warning that the name is already taken (at least for inside this window).

8. Drag untitled folder 2 onto My New Folder.

9. Open My New Folder and rename untitled folder 2 to My New Folder. This name is acceptable, because no other item at its level has that name.

10. Rename this nested folder to *My Newer Folder.*

11. Create another new folder here and name it *My Newest Folder* (see fig. 8.18).

Figure 8.18
*After creating My
Newest Folder.*

Dragging Folders in Different Views

1. If it's not already there, drag My Newest Folder into My New Folder.

2. Close all windows except for the hard disk window.

3. Change view to by Name.

4. Click on the arrow next to My New Folder to see the organization of your new folders in outline form (see fig. 8.19).

Figure 8.19
*Outline text view of
new folders.*

5. Drag My Newest Folder to the following places in the order indicated:

   a. The Desktop. It leaves the hard disk window entirely and turns into an icon.

   b. Any place in the hard disk window where another folder does *not* highlight. This places My Newest Folder at the root level.

   c. Into My New Folder. It goes to the same level as My Newer Folder.

   d. Into My Newer Folder. Now it is as fully nested as it can be in this location.

Moving a Folder of Stuff

1. Drag My New Folder to the Desktop. Everything inside that folder came along with it.

2. Open My New Folder and My Newer Folder.

3. In turn, drag My Newest Folder and My Newer Folder to the Desktop and then close all windows related to these folders (see fig. 8.20).

Figure 8.20
*New folders dragged
to the Desktop turn
into large icon style.*

Moving Multiple Items

1. Hold down the Shift key and click on each of the three folders. Each one stays selected.

2. Release the Shift key and place the pointer on any one of the selected folders. Drag the folder to the hard disk icon. All three folders go into the hard disk window and remain selected (see fig. 8.21).

Figure 8.21
Dragging all three selected items to the hard disk.

3. Drag all three as a group to the Trash icon. We'll discuss the Trash in the next chapter.

Setting Up Your Desktop

1. Unless you've been instructed by someone to follow another organization method, begin by making sure that your hard disk root directory contains at least these three folders: System Folder (it's probably already there with the special symbol in the folder icon), Applications, and Documents.

> **Performa owners note:** Drag the special Documents folder to the hard disk window.

2. All other items in this root level should go inside these three folders. For example, if you see a folder labeled with the name of a program you recognize (e.g., Microsoft Word), drag this entire folder into the

Applications folder. Select and check the Get Info dialog for any files you don't recognize by name or icon. Applications should go into the Applications folder; documents should go into the Documents folder. If you find other unknown kinds of files (such as things called aliases), leave them at the root for now but drag them to the bottom of the window.

3. Resize the hard disk window so that you see only the three folders, as shown in figure 8.22.

Figure 8.22
Suggested size, layout, and contents of your hard disk window.

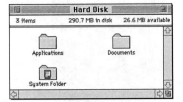

4. If it's not already set this way, set the view of the hard disk window to Icon.

5. Open the Applications folder and set the view to Name. Do the same for the Documents folder.

6. Resize and position the Applications and Documents windows as shown in figure 8.23.

7. Close all windows.

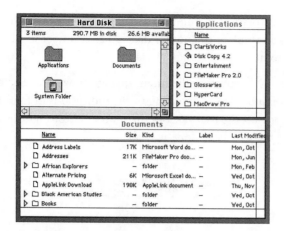

Figure 8.23
Suggested layout of primary Desktop windows. Each window reopens to its previous size and location.

Summary

In this encounter, we've learned how to manipulate folders and files to create an effective organization method for the documents we'll be creating. We've also seen how to use the Get Info dialog box to uncover information about any item we see on the Desktop or in a folder window.

Exorcises

1. Name at least two ways to determine whether a file is an application or document.

2. What can you determine about the contents of the Letters folder in figure 8.24?

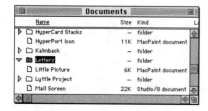

Figure 8.24
What's in the Letters folder?

3. Describe the two fastest methods of moving a file deeply nested inside your Applications folder to another deeply nested folder inside your Documents folder.

4. In the following illustration, the intention is to move the selected file to the *Applications* folder. According to the indications in figure 8.25, what will happen if the user releases the mouse button right now? What should the user have done instead?

Figure 8.25
Where is the dragged file going?

Staying Organized

Goal
Learn skills important to maintaining an organized Macintosh, including ways of finding deeply nested files and clearing away unneeded files.

What You Will Need
Macintosh turned on, showing the Desktop.

Terms of Enfearment
Find
Find Again
pop-up menu
copying files
Trash

Briefing
Where's That #&%* File?

After a hard disk gets lots of files and folders stored on it, we can use the Finder to help us locate a particular file. Interestingly, it wasn't until Version 7 of the System Software that the Finder actually performed any *finding*.

The simplest search method is to ask the Finder to look for a match of a file or folder name (or portion thereof). In the File menu is a *Find* command, which leads to a dialog box (see fig. 9.1). Type any series of letters that will help the Finder narrow down the search among all items on the volumes currently mounted on the Desktop. Press Return or click the Find button to start the search process.

Figure 9.1

Choosing Find in the Finder's File menu leads to a dialog box for entering a name to search.

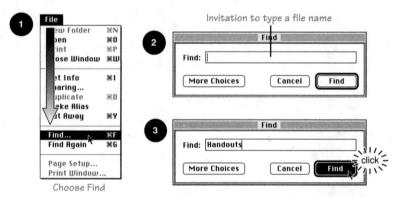

When the search fails to find a match, a dialog box alerts us of the fact. If the Finder locates a match, it opens up that item's window, scrolls to the item, and selects the item to distinguish it from the rest (see fig. 9.2).

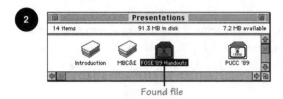

Found file

Figure 9.2
*If searching takes
more than a couple
of seconds, we see the
progress dialog box.
Then the window
opens, and the
matching file icon is
selected.*

Eureka! (Almost)

It is very possible that the item located by the Finder isn't the exact item
we're looking for, even though it meets the name criteria we specified in
the Find dialog. The Finder remembers the last item it searched for, so
we can issue the *Find Again* command (also in the File menu) to let the
Finder continue through the volume(s) in search of another match (see
fig. 9.3). When it cannot find another matching item, a system beep sound
informs us.

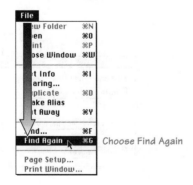

Choose Find Again

Figure 9.3
*If the first match
isn't the one we
want, we choose
Find Again to look
for the next match.*

Advanced Searching

We can get even more specific about what the Finder should look for. That's what the More Choices button in the Find dialog leads to. The expanded Find dialog box contains a few *pop-up menus*—menus that behave much like menu bar menus but that are positioned in the middle of a window. Clicking and holding down on the top left menu, for instance, shows that Finder searches by a wide array of attributes (see fig. 9.4). As an example, we can search for all files whose modification date is today's date—files we may want to duplicate for safety (see fig. 9.5).

By clicking the all at once checkbox, we instruct the Finder to not only find all matches, but to temporarily turn the hard disk window into a Text view and then to select all matching files (see fig. 9.6). If a matching file is

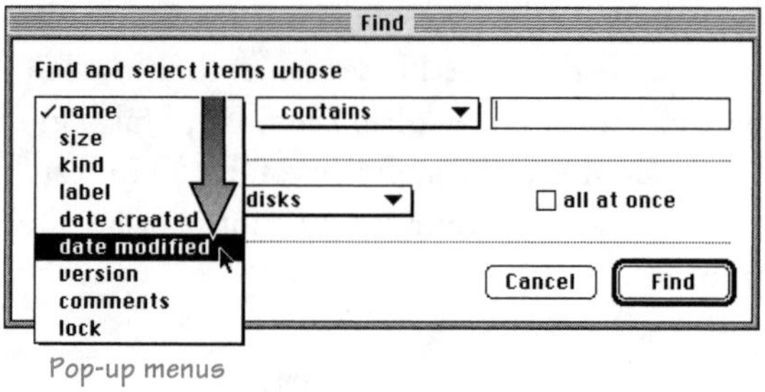

Figure 9.4
We can get more specific in our search criteria with these additional choices.

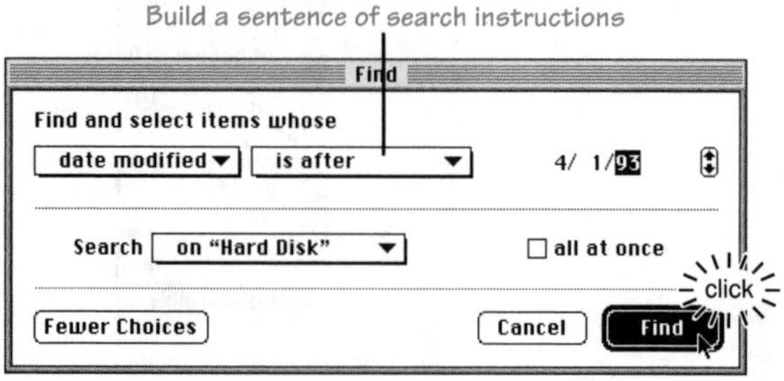

Pop-up menus

Figure 9.5
This search will locate all files that have been modified after April 1, 1993.

Build a sentence of search instructions

nested some levels deep inside folders, the Finder expands those folder list views so that the found file can be selected. With all those files selected at once, we can drag the bunch of them by dragging any one of them—just like Shift-clicking to select multiple items (see fig. 9.7).

Figure 9.6

The all at once *checkbox selects all found files in a text view of the hard disk.*

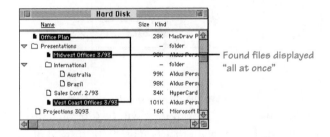

Found files displayed "all at once"

Figure 9.7

An all at once *search for the word "office" yields at least three matches we can see.*

Copying Files

In all the dragging of files and folders up to now, all we were doing was moving items around. When we're done, there is still one copy of each file on the disk. We can, however, make a copy of a file on the hard disk—in two ways, no less.

The first way is to select the item in a Finder window and then to choose Duplicate from the File menu. This method creates a copy bearing the name of the original file, plus the word "copy" as part of the name (see fig. 9.8). (We can't have two files of the same name at the same level, right?)

Figure 9.8

One way to create a second copy of an item is to select it and then choose Duplicate. The duplicate has the same name plus "copy."

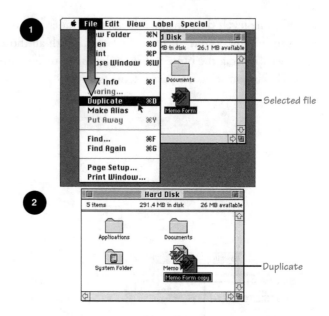

Selected file

Duplicate

When the copy of a file we're making is supposed to go into another folder on the same hard disk, we can use a speedcut. Hold down the Option key while dragging an item from one folder to another (see fig. 9.9). Instead of just moving the item, the Finder duplicates the selected file and puts the copy—with the exact same name as the original in the destination.

Figure 9.9

Option-dragging to another folder copies an item. The copy retains the same name as the original.

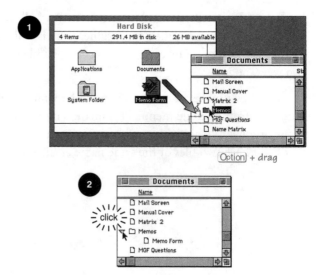

Duplicating files on the hard disk is actually a disk-space-wasteful thing to do. As we'll learn later, the Finder lets us create very small stand-in files that represent a file or folder when multiple copies of them would be convenient. *Aliases*, as they're known, come in quite handy.

We're more likely to want to make a copy of a file or folder for storage on another hard disk, file server, or even a floppy disk volume. The Finder simplifies that as well, and we'll get to it in the 17th Encounter, in which we discuss sharing information via floppy disk.

Trash

The wastebasket in your office isn't really the final resting ground for something you throw out. In fact, you can still rummage around in there to retrieve an accidentally discarded item until the basket is emptied (when it goes into serious trash that gets picked up for the dump). The Macintosh *Trash* works the same way as your wastebasket.

To remove a file or folder from a Finder window, we drag its icon to the Trash. To let us know something is in the Trash, its icon changes to a bulging can (see fig. 9.10). The item isn't actually deleted from the hard disk until we empty the trash—choose Empty Trash from the Special menu. Thus, if you're trying to open up space on the hard disk by dragging un-wanted items to the Trash, nothing changes in the hard disk's in disk and available legends until you empty the Trash (see fig. 9.11). Until then, you can open the Trash just like any volume and drag an item back onto the Desktop or into some other folder.

As a way of protecting us from accidental erasure, the Finder warns us each time we choose Empty Trash from the Special menu. After a short time, this warning only gets in our way. As a speedcut, select the Trash icon and choose Get Info from the File menu. Uncheck the checkbox at the bottom of the Trash's Get Info dialog to put an end to that annoying dialog each time we empty the Trash (see fig. 9.12).

Figure 9.10

Dragging an item to the Trash icon is like throwing something into a wastebasket. The Trash fattens when something is in it and still retrievable.

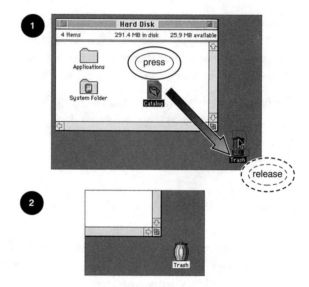

Different from DOS

Without the help of a disk-management utility program, it is impossible to move discontinuous groups of files from one subdirectory to another, as you can with Macintosh files and folders. Straight DOS also doesn't have any file-searching capabilities. Moving or deleting any item requires a lengthy command, including the precarious pathname.

Figure 9.11

Emptying the Trash opens up disk space occupied by items we've previously discarded.

Figure 9.12
*We can eliminate
the trash warning in
the Trash's Get Info
dialog box.*

They're Out To Get Us

Although Finder searches are quite helpful, they can leave our Finder windows and Desktop in a mess. After a successful search, the last matching window is left open, even if no more are found with the Find Again command. Moreover, if we choose the all at once option, the Finder leaves our view of the hard disk root in a text listing. Restoration to an iconic view is up to us.

After the Trash is emptied, nothing that comes with the Macintosh will dig a file out of the dump. Some commercial software programs, however, can attempt to recover a deleted file. (The file isn't erased, only its entry in the hard disk's internal table of contents.)

Before dragging a folder to the Trash, always check that you intend everything in the folder is to be thrown out—the Finder can't read your mind. The phrase, "I didn't mean that one, too!" falls on deaf chips.

The Finder does, however, prevent us from tossing a document into the Trash while a program still has it open. A gentle dialog reminds us of our attempted error (see fig. 9.13). Clicking the Continue button tells the Mac to finish emptying the rest of the Trash if there are more files there.

Figure 9.13
Files still open in an application can't be trashed. The Continue choice carries on other Trash duties.

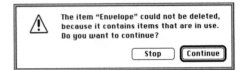

The item "Envelope" could not be deleted, because it contains items that are in use. Do you want to continue?

Stop   Continue

Practice

Unsuccessful Search

1. Choose Find from the File menu.

2. Enter "ABC123" and press Return, which is the same as clicking the highlighted Find button in the dialog (see fig. 9.14). An alert box tells of an unsuccessful search.

Figure 9.14
Search for "ABC123."

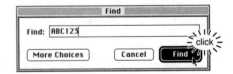

Find

Find: ABC123

More Choices   Cancel   Find

click

A Successful Search

1. Choose Find from the File menu.

2. Enter "System Folder" and press Return (see fig. 9.15). The Finder locates the System Folder icon and selects it.

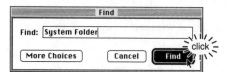

Figure 9.15
Search for "System Folder."

3. Choose Find Again to hear the beep that occurs when only one match has been found.

Continued Searching

1. Search for the word "Folder."

2. Choose Find Again from the File menu (see fig. 9.16).

Figure 9.16
Choosing Find Again.

3. Continue choosing Find Again (or typing Command-G) until you reach the end.

Duplicating an Item

1. Create a folder at the root level and name it *Encounter 9 Folder*.

2. Click anywhere in the white space of the window to deselect the new folder.

3. Pull down the File menu and notice that because no item is selected, the Duplicate command is dimmed.

4. Click once on the *Encounter 9 Folder* to select it.

5. Choose Duplicate from the File menu.

6. Drag the *Encounter 9 Folder* folder onto the Documents folder.

7. Open the Documents folder and rename the new folder like its original, *Encounter 9 Folder* (see fig. 9.17).

Figure 9.17
Naming a folder.

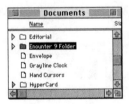

8. Close the Documents Folder

Duplication Speedcut

1. Option-drag the original *Encounter 9 Folder* to the Applications folder.

2. Open the Applications folder to see the results of the option-drag.

3. Close the Applications folder.

Basic Searching

1. Choose Find from the File menu, enter Encounter 9, and press Return.

2. Continue choosing Find Again until the Finder beeps that there are no more matches. Along the way, watch the windows the Finder opens in looking for *Encounter 9* matches.

3. Close all windows except the hard disk window.

More Sophisticated Searching

1. Choose Find from the File menu.

2. Click the More Choices button to reveal the expanded search dialog.

3. Check the `all at once` checkbox and click the Find button (see fig. 9.18).

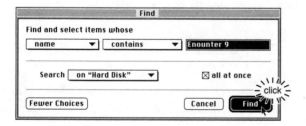

Figure 9.18
Begin an `all at once` *search for Encounter 9.*

4. Scroll up and down the hard disk window to see where the three selected Encounter 9 Folders are located (see fig. 9.19).

Figure 9.19
Scroll up and down to find the three found files.

5. Drag the selected items (by dragging just one) to the Desktop. An alert dialog reminds you that you cannot have multiple items with the same name in the same place. The items go back to their original positions, still selected.

Dragging to the Trash

1. Drag the selected Encounter 9 Folders en masse to the Trash. An alert tells you that you can't drag all of them to the Trash at once because they all have the same name.

2. Use the Find command with the all at once checkbox unchecked to locate the first Encounter 9 folder.

3. Drag the found folder to the Trash.

4. Use the Find Again command (Command-G) to locate the other two copies of this folder. Drag each one to the Trash.

5. Open the Trash window to see how the Trash handles multiple items of the same name when dragged one-by-one (see fig. 9.20).

Figure 9.20
How the Trash accommodates same-named files.

Trash Warning

1. Drag one Encounter 9 Folder icon to the Desktop.

2. Choose Empty Trash from the Special menu. If the menu item ends in an ellipsis (meaning that a dialog will result), the trash warning alert appears; click OK.

3. Click once on the Trash icon and choose Get Info from the File menu.

4. Uncheck the `warn before emptying` checkbox.

5. Drag the Encounter 9 Folder from the Desktop into the Trash.

6. Choose Empty Trash from the Special menu (notice in figure 9.21 that the menu item no longer displays an ellipsis). The Trash icon returns to its unchubby self.

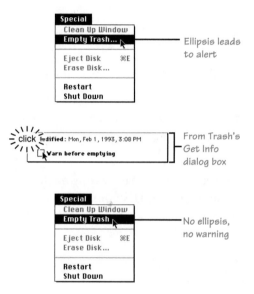

Figure 9.21
Changing the status of the Trash's warn before emptying *checkbox affects the Empty Trash command in the Special menu.*

7. Decide which trash emptying method you prefer, mark the `warn before emptying` checkbox accordingly and close the Get Info dialog box.

8. Close the Trash window.

Summary

The Finder actually finds—letting us search our hard disk(s) for files or folders whose exact location we don't remember. We saw the difference between moving files around a volume and making copies of them on the same volume, including the Option-drag-and-drop shortcut for placing a copy of a file into another folder. The Trash icon is only a temporary holding place for unneeded files—they can be dragged out of the Trash until the Empty Trash command pulverizes the items into dust.

Exorcises

1. Describe the two fastest ways to place a copy of a file into another folder.

2. Suppose that your hard disk is getting full and that you want to open up some space. Detail the steps you would go through to accomplish this.

3. You want to archive all the work you've done today by copying those files to another volume (whose icon is on your Desktop). What would be the most expedient way to accomplish this?

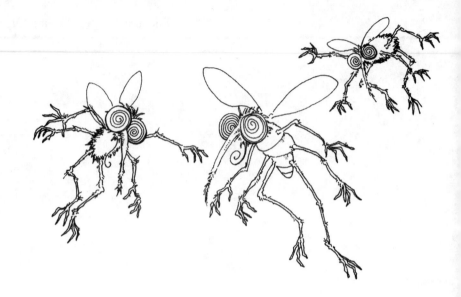

Starting a Program

Goal

Become acquainted with ways to start a program, learn how to switch between multiple programs for maximum efficiency, and recognize which program is running at any moment.

What You Will Need

Macintosh turned on, showing the Desktop. A program called TeachText installed on your hard disk (the Macintosh System Software installation process does this for you).

Terms of Enfearment

program	launching
application	palette
desk accessory (DA)	toolbar
booting	TeachText

Briefing

Everything you've learned so far is vital to using the Macintosh, but little of it has anything to do with the work you do. What turns the Mac into a practical tool for your daily labors is a *program*. Each program transforms the collection of computer parts into a special-purpose tool for writing, massaging budgets, organizing information, drafting, and so on—virtually everything that involves knowledge, facts, or ideas.

The terms *program* and *application* are often used interchangeably; the latter sounds less computer-like. Sometimes, the terms are used together, as in *application program*, to distinguish an application from other kinds of programs (e.g., a *utility program* that backs up a hard disk). Gurus usually shorten the word application to just plain *app*.

Two Program Types

A Macintosh program can be either a *desk accessory* (DA) or a full-fledged application program. Like the stapler and paper clip cup on your real desk, Macintosh desk accessories are readily available (you choose them from the ubiquitous Apple menu shown in fig. 10.1) and serve a highly targeted purpose. Several desk accessories come with the Macintosh, including a handy calculator, simple alarm clock, and a note pad to jot down notes. In guru-speak, a desk accessory is referred to by the acronym DA.

Figure 10.1
Desk accessories are listed in the Apple menu.

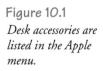

Apple desk accessories

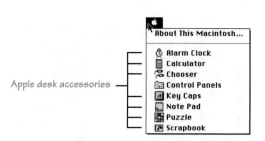

Full-fledged applications are the ones that you use for your real work. They're the word processors, spreadsheets, databases, communications, and graphics programs that help you cope with all kinds of information. (Many clever programmers have also reduced these functions to small desk accessory programs, but most of the mainstream productivity programs are regular applications.)

Purchased commercial programs arrive on floppy disks. To use a program, you usually copy it to the hard disk, often by way of an automatic installer (installation instructions vary from program to program). When installed on your hard disk, the program consists of one or more files, one of which is the one you start from the Finder. The Macintosh also lets you place any application into the Apple menu, as you'll see later.

Starting a Desk Accessory

All it takes to start up a desk accessory is to choose it from the Apple menu. A DA usually generates a window of some kind, in which the program lets you work with it. The menu bar also changes to one that applies only to the desk accessory (see fig. 10.2). Generally speaking, desk accessory menu bars provide modified File and Edit menus, plus perhaps one program-specific menu to the right of the Edit menu.

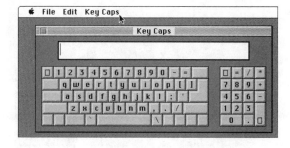

Figure 10.2
A desk accessory, like KeyCaps, appears in its own window and takes over the menu bar.

A couple of other indicators show you when a desk accessory is running. The name of the DA is listed in the Application menu (see fig. 10.3). Moreover, the first item in the Apple menu changes to the word "About" plus the name of the DA (see fig. 10.4). Choosing this menu item displays a dialog box with author and copyright information.

Figure 10.3
An open DA appears as a program in the Application menu. The checkmark signifies the topmost (active) program on-screen.

Calculator DA listed as an application

Figure 10.4
A DA also changes the first item in the Apple menu.

DA Behavior

Desk accessories are as reliable as any application, but they do behave slightly differently. For starters, they generally have only one window. If you close that window, you also quit the program—taking you back to the program you were running before (see fig. 10.5). If you've entered some information into the window, the DA will either save the information automatically or ask you whether you want to save it.

Figure 10.5
Closing a desk accessory's window is the same as quitting from the DA's File menu.

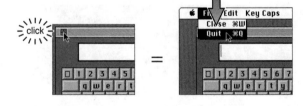

Starting an Application

Although starting an application is easy, remembering all the terms for it may not be. You'll hear phrases like *booting* or *loading* the program and *launching* the app (or any combination). They all mean the same thing: starting the application.

Starting an application is as easy as double-clicking on the program's icon in the Finder, in any Finder window view style you like (see fig. 10.6). This action is the same as selecting the icon and choosing Open from the Finder's File menu (here's another way to describe the action: *opening* an application).

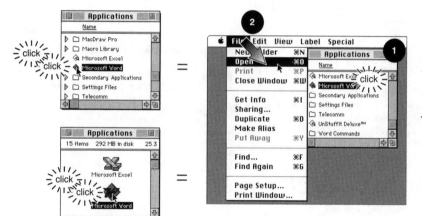

Figure 10.6
Double-clicking an application icon produces the same result as selecting it and choosing Open from the File menu: the program launches. We can double-click in icon or text views.

Programs usually take several seconds longer to get going than DAs do, but when they're ready, the same kind of things happen on the screen. The menu bar changes but usually with many more program-specific menus showing (see fig. 10.7). In the Application menu, the program's name is listed (see fig. 10.8), and the first item in the Apple menu says "About" plus the name of the program.

Figure 10.7
Applications usually offer more application-specific menus than DAs. Here is Microsoft Word's menu bar.

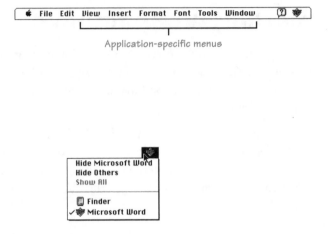

Application-specific menus

Figure 10.8
All open applications appear in the Application menu.

Performa users' note: The Launcher window provided in Performa models is another facility for keeping applications handy on the Desktop and available for quick launching. A single click of a program icon in the Launcher window starts the program.

Program Behavior

Applications can often display multiple windows (although only one blank one appears when you start the program). Some programs also display one or more additional smaller windows, called *palettes*. Found more in graphics-oriented programs, palettes contain tools that let us switch between types of operations, such as typing text, drawing circles, or dragging chunks of our work around the window. The precise functions of palettes vary from program to program, and the palette window style may also vary, but you can drag them around by their title bars and close them by clicking their close boxes, just like Finder windows seen earlier.

Figure 10.9
Some programs provide palette windows that float above other windows. This is a HyperCard navigation palette.

An increasingly popular feature appearing in program screens is the *toolbar*. It usually extends across the screen just below the menu bar. It may also appear inside a window. Toolbars display icons that represent frequently used pull-down menu commands (see fig. 10.10). You can click them as a speedcut to dragging through a menu.

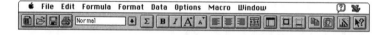

Figure 10.10
Toolbars, like this one from Microsoft Excel, present one-click icon shortcuts for frequently accessed menu items.

Using Multiple Programs

The Macintosh accommodates as many programs as the machine has available RAM space. Desk accessories take up less than 32K, but large applications can try to grab 2,000K or more.

Even though more than one program can be open, only one can be the active program—the one whose menu bar appears across the screen. Other programs may actually be performing some action in the background (such as sending a file to another computer over the telephone), but only one application can be on top of the pile visually.

That active application is the one bearing the checkmark in the Application menu—the menu we also use to switch from one application to another (see fig. 10.11). Whichever program we choose becomes the front-most, active application. Another way to bring an application to the front is to click on any window belonging to that program.

Figure 10.11

One way to change between open applications is to choose one in the Application menu. The checkmark denotes the active program.

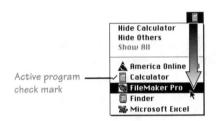

Active program check mark

Different from DOS

Starting a program from the DOS `c:\>` prompt usually means remembering the name of the EXE or batch file that starts the program, so you can type it at the prompt. All Macintosh programs start the same way: with a double-click of an icon.

Desk accessories correspond to TSR (terminate-and-stay-resident) programs in DOS. TSRs tend to pop up more quickly than loading DAs, but Macintosh DAs integrate more fully with other applications, such as copying a calculator result and pasting it into any application running at the same time. In fact, the Macintosh excels at the ease of copying information between different applications, because the consistency of underlying functions is inherent in the system software—not the case at all in DOS, in which each program has its own way of handling information.

They're Out To Get Us

Unless your Macintosh has gobs of RAM installed, you will inevitably encounter a low-memory alert when you try to open one more program than the machine has RAM for. If the Macintosh detects that you are not using a program (i.e., the program has no windows open), a dialog box offers to quit that program to open up some RAM for the one you want to activate (see fig. 10.12). Although the Mac is pretty smart about managing RAM, you can do some things to help it along. These techniques are discussed in the 21st Encounter.

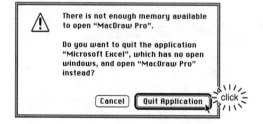

Figure 10.12
Programs require memory to run, so you may run low if you try to open lots of them. The Mac tries to help open up memory when needed.

Although I said earlier that you can click on an inactive program's window to activate that program, it is possible that one program's window will become totally hidden by another application's window (see fig. 10.13). This situation is not really a problem, because you can use the Application menu to make that otherwise hidden window come to the top of the pile.

Figure 10.13
*Clicking a large
window from an
inactive program
may hide a smaller
one. You can move
the windows around
or reactivate the
program via the
Application menu.*

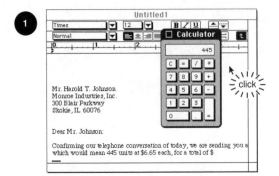

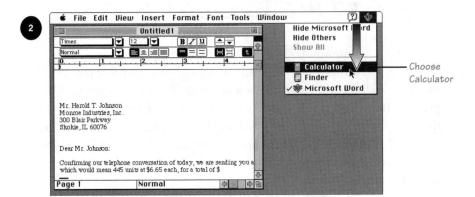

Choose
Calculator

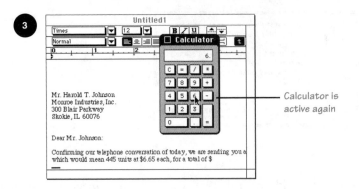

Calculator is
active again

A Clean Screen

If things get too confusing on the screen with all kinds of applications showing, use the Hide Others command in the Application menu to hide all but the active application. Selecting this command doesn't quit those programs—it just temporarily hides them from view. Hidden programs' icons are dimmed in the Application menu, but you can choose one to bring it back into view (see fig. 10.14).

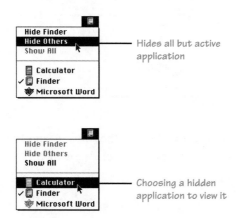

Figure 10.14
You can hide all but the active application to keep the screen clean. Hidden program icons are dimmed in the Application menu, but choosing any one makes it visible and active.

Note, however, that when the Finder is the active application, only its windows appear in front of other programs' windows. Desktop icons stay all the way at the bottom of the pile and may be hidden by windows from inactive programs (see fig. 10.15). Choose Hide Others from the Application menu to reveal those icons.

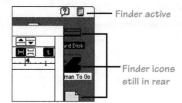

Figure 10.15
Even when the Finder is the active program (see its small icon at the top of the Application menu), Desktop icons stay behind any program windows that may be open.

Practice

Check Out Your DAs

1. From the Desktop, open the Hard Disk window and locate the System Folder (see fig. 10.16).

Figure 10.16
Locate the System Folder.

2. Open the System Folder and locate the Apple Menu Items folder; this folder contains items that appear in the Apple menu (see fig. 10.17).

3. Open the Apple Menu Items folder.

Figure 10.17
Apple Menu Items folder.

4. Pull down the View menu and set the view of this window to by Kind (see fig. 10.18). Items listed as desk accessories are the ones installed in your Mac. You could start one by double-clicking on its icon, but because the folder is usually closed when you use the Mac, it's easier to start them from the Apple menu.

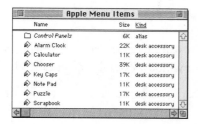

Figure 10.18
Apple Menu Items folder sorted by Kind.

5. Close the Apple Menu Items and System folders.

Start a Desk Accessory

1. Choose Calculator from the Apple menu (see fig. 10.19).

Figure 10.19
Open the Calculator desk accessory.

2. Choose About Calculator from the Apple menu. Click on the OK button in the dialog box.

3. Pull down the File and Edit menus and notice how the menus contain just the basic File and Edit commands, which are all that are needed for this desk accessory.

4. Pull down the Application menu and notice that Calculator is added to the list of applications.

Using the Desk Accessory

1. Drag the Calculator window to the right of the screen so that some or all of the Calculator window extends beyond the Hard Disk window.

2. Enter some information into the calculator by clicking on the buttons in the window or using the numeric keypad (if you have one).

Switching between a DA and the Finder

1. Click inside the Hard Disk window. Notice how the menu bar has changed back to the Finder's menus.

2. Pull down the Application menu and see that the Finder is now the active application.

Starting an Application

1. Locate *TeachText* on your hard disk (either search manually by opening folders or, more efficiently, use the Find command in the File menu).

2. Double-click the TeachText icon (see fig. 10.20). The program appears to zoom out from the icon.

Figure 10.20
Launching TeachText with a double-click.

3. Pull down the Apple, File, Edit, and Application menus to see how they've changed with TeachText as the active application.

Switching among Programs

1. Use the Application menu to activate Calculator.

2. Choose Hide Others from the Application menu. Notice how all other windows (but not the Finder's icons) disappear.

3. Pull down the Application menu and see how icons (but not the names) of hidden programs are dimmed.

4. Choose TeachText from the Application menu to activate it.

5. Click back and forth between the TeachText window and the Calculator window, watching the menu bar change as each program becomes the active program.

6. Choose Show All from the Application menu to bring all open programs' windows from hiding (see fig. 10.21); the order of programs does not change.

Figure 10.21
Showing all hidden programs (the Finder has a dimmed icon and will appear when this command is carried out).

Showing Just the Finder

1. Click anywhere on the Desktop pattern to make the Finder the active application.

2. Choose Hide Others from the Application menu. The Finder is the only application showing, giving you easy access to all windows and icons.

3. Choose Show All from the Applications menu.

Summary

Two kinds of Macintosh programs—desk accessories and applications—share a number of important attributes, particularly in the way they take over the menu bar and are listed in the Application menu. DAs are listed in the Apple menu for easy starting, and applications can be double-clicked to start. You can open as many DAs and programs as your Macintosh has available RAM and then freely switch among programs as you need them.

Exorcises

1. Describe the similarities between a desk accessory and an application.

2. Describe the differences between a desk accessory and an application.

3. Detail the steps in each of three ways to change from an open application to an open desk accessory.

4. Describe two ways to find out which desk accessory or application is the active program.

5. What does the menu in figure 10.22 tell you about the programs on this Macintosh?

Figure 10.22
What's the situation with these applications?

| Hide Information Manager |
| Hide Others |
| Show All |
| |
| Classic Trilogy™ |
| Finder |
| ✓ Information Manager |
| MacRATT |

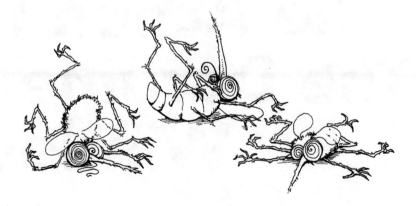

Where the Action Is: The Document Window

Goal

Examine where we do the real work with the computer—the document window.

What You Will Need

Where we left Encounter 10, with the Macintosh turned on and TeachText open.

Terms of Enfearment

document
document window
spreadsheet
graphics program
database
text editor

Briefing

Document Terminology

Unless you dwell in the Realm of Pure Thought, your work produces something tangible. Perhaps it's on paper, from a tiny doodle to a multi-volume encyclopedia; perhaps the work ultimately becomes a color slide for a presentation; it even may be an audio or video tape of material you or others recorded. To the Macintosh, each chunk of work, stored on the hard disk as a separate file, is called a *document*.

The less a program replicates printed documents from the real world, the more likely it will have its own terminology for a document. For instance, a document that contains a video sequence may be called a *movie* or a *clip* in a video-editing program. Such naming helps users experienced with those terms make the connection between the real world and what's taking place on the Mac. To the Mac, however, a document is a document, regardless of its content.

The Document Workplace

All work on a document takes place in a *document window*. The precise look of a document window varies widely with the application. It may be a completely blank canvas for drawing, a grid of rectangles for entering numbers in a ledger-like sheet, or a well-defined form that needs to be filled out blank-by-blank (see fig. 11.1). In designing Macintosh document windows, a program's creator usually tries to replicate in electronic form something familiar from the real world.

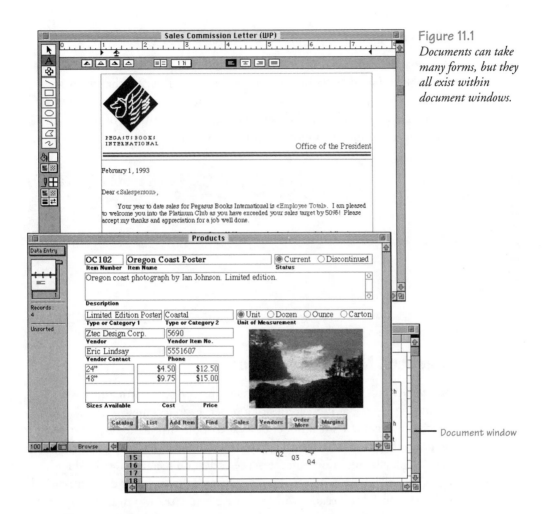

Figure 11.1
Documents can take many forms, but they all exist within document windows.

Document window

A New Document

When most programs start, they present a new, untitled document window. This is the equivalent of the dreaded blank sheet of paper lying before you on the desk. Despite powerful tools available in the program, it is up to us to do the next step: put something into the document. Here are some examples.

Text Entry

Any document that expects lots of text (e.g., word processing) awaits typing from the keyboard. A flashing text insertion pointer tells us that the next characters we type on the keyboard will go where the pointer is flashing (see fig. 11.2). Setting margins, line spacing, and other attributes of the document are left to menu commands or tool bar clicks.

Figure 11.2
In this word processor window, the text insertion pointer flashes where the next character we type will appear. (Microsoft Word)

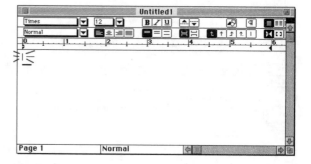

Numbers, Numbers, Numbers

Spreadsheet programs are popular, because they present a structured way of organizing figures, as if on accounting paper. Each rectangle is called a cell, which can contain a raw number or a calculation formula to be performed on raw numbers of other cells (e.g., the total for a column of figures). In place of the text insertion pointer is a cell selection rectangle, which highlights the cell whose contents are to be changed. Spreadsheet data entry is stranger than most, because you type into a text entry area near the top of the window (see fig. 11.3). Only when you press the Tab, Return, or Enter key does what you type officially get entered into the selected cell.

Figure 11.3
Entry of information into spreadsheet cells is usually by way of a data-entry field.

A Thousand Words

The specifics about working with *graphics programs* vary widely from program to program. One basic methodology holds for nearly all of them: you choose a tool from a palette, the pointer becomes that tool, and you then start drawing in the document window with that tool (see fig. 11.4). One tool might draw straight lines, and another may draw ovals filled with color patterns. There is no insertion pointer or selected cell—we control every aspect of a shape's location with the mouse-controlled pointer.

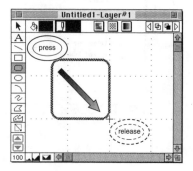

Figure 11.4

In this MacDraw Pro document, we choose a tool (round rectangle) and then drag the shape with the mouse.

A Base of Data

At many times in our lives, we've kept lists of information. The data may have been so voluminous as to require a shoe box full of index cards or short enough to be written on a small note paper in our wallets. The larger a collection of data becomes, the more helpful a computer is, because the computer is quick at sorting and finding what we want. There are two parts to a *database* program: designing the database and entering and working with information in the database. The former is the more difficult of the tasks but is required before any information may be entered (see fig. 11.5). After the database is set up, however, it is a piece of cake to enter additional information into the database's on-screen forms, as shown in figure 11.6, and to extract information based on selection criteria (e.g., all sales prospects whose telephone numbers contain the 212 area code).

Figure 11.5

*Before we enter
information into a
database, we must
design a form layout,
with each field's
name, location, and
size. (ClarisWorks)*

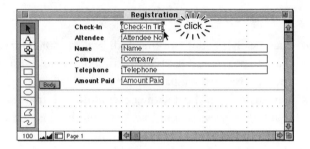

Figure 11.6

*After the layout is
set, we can begin
filling in data.
(ClarisWorks)*

If You Don't Know How To Start

If you come to a program and you're at a loss about what to do next, here are some things to try:

1. Type a few characters on the keyboard. If the program is ready to edit text, you'll see the characters in the document window.

2. Browse through the menus looking for a command that starts with the word "New." This command should get some action.

3. Look for a tools palette. Click on a tool, move the pointer into the document window, and click and drag the tool around the page. If there is no tools palette, but there is a Window menu, pull down that menu to see whether there is a Tools palette that can be shown.

4. Look to the File menu for unusual commands that lead to dialog boxes. Programs that rely on existing documents (such as desktop publishing programs) may have special menu items that let you bring in a document for further manipulation. For example, PageMaker's File menu offers the Place command.

5. The last resort is to go to the program's manual. We'll have more to say about that later.

Document Window Elements

All the elements we've learned about Finder windows—title bar, close box, zoom box, grow box, and scroll bars—can appear in document windows (see fig. 11.7). Their behavior is identical to Finder window elements. Don't be surprised if one or more elements is missing because they don't apply to the particular kind of document you're working on.

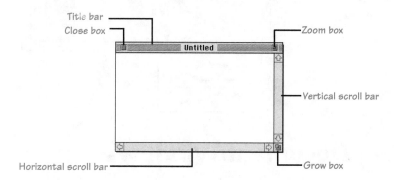

Figure 11.7
Document windows typically have the same controls as Finder windows.

You may, however, see additional elements. These vary from program to program, although each software publisher tends to reuse several elements to help make their products appear to be in the same family. Recent programs can give you on-screen assistance with unknown window elements when you turn on Balloon Help. Choose Show Balloons from the Help menu and roll the pointer atop an unidentified element (see fig. 11.8). A cartoon-like balloon offers a brief explanation of what that item does when you click on or drag it.

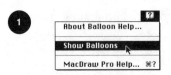

Figure 11.8
Choosing Show Balloons lets a Help system tell us what unknown window elements do. Just roll the pointer atop an item to see its explanation.

Closing Document Windows

Clicking the close box (or choosing Close Window, when available in the File menu) closes the active window (see fig. 11.9). Most programs are smart enough to know when we've made any changes to the content of a window and will ask us whether changes should be saved before the window closes. The dialog box may look something like figure 11.10.

Figure 11.9
Clicking a document window's close box.

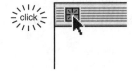

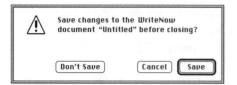

Figure 11.10
Mac software warns us if we try to close a document without saving changes.

Read this alert carefully and be sure to understand the impact of each button choice. The Save button lets us store the document to the hard disk (which we'll discuss fully in the next lesson). The Cancel button is also safe, because it cancels the window closing process. It lets us take back the Close Window command.

By far the most dangerous button is the Don't Save one, because it closes the window and blows away anything we've done since the last time we saved the document (which may have been never, if we just started with a blank document window).

Multiple Documents

Most programs allow us to open more than one document window at a time to facilitate flipping between documents or copying a chunk from one to another. To find out if a program you're using allows multiple documents, pull down the File menu when one document window is already open. If the Open command is active, you can open another without closing the active document (see fig. 11.11). The maximum number of windows allowed by the program usually depends on the amount of memory your program occupies and how memory-hungry each document is.

Figure 11.11
Many programs allow multiple documents opened at the same time. Check for an active Open command while a document window is already opened.

Like everything else in the Macintosh, however, only one document window is active at any given moment. The active document window is the one on top of the pile with a title bar displaying horizontal lines.

Different from DOS

Except when using Microsoft Windows, DOS program documents tend to occupy the entire screen, rather than a window area on the screen. If multiple documents can be opened at the same time in the program, activating a specific document may require cycling through all open documents to reach the one you want.

They're Out To Get Us

Although palettes and tool bars are supposedly there to help us work with a program, some programs really overdo a good thing. The result is a confusing array of incomprehensible icons and a series of small windows that do more obstructing than helping. On smaller screen Macintoshes, all these windows can become a screen real-estate management problem.

Although document and Finder windows share lots of good things, the same
cautions apply, as well. Smaller windows can be completely obscured by
activating larger windows. Typically, a Window menu provides a list of all
open windows, and we can choose the one we want to become active (see fig.
11.12). In absence of such a menu, it may be necessary to resize or drag the
larger window to reveal the smaller one.

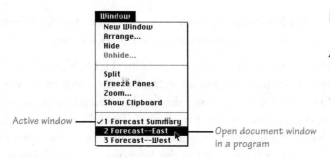

Figure 11.12
*When available, a
program's Window
menu helps us
manage multiple
document windows.*

Active window

Open document window
in a program

Practice

Document Window Calisthenics

1. With TeachText running and a document window showing, drag the
   grow box to resize the window as shown in figure 11.13.

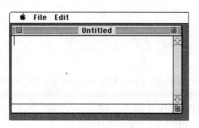

Figure 11.13
*Resize the TechText
document window.*

2. Click the zoom box. Notice how the window zooms to fill the screen
   except for a sliver that shows Hard Disk and Trash icons on the
   Desktop underneath.

3. Click the zoom box again to bring the window back to the resized state.

4. Drag the window around the screen with its title bar.

Entering Information

1. Type a long sentence, such as the time-worn favorite: Now is the time for all good men to come to the aid of their country.

2. Resize the window as shown in figure 11.14. Notice how TeachText treats this text: margins are defined by the width of the window. Word processors normally don't do this (but TeachText is just a simple *text editor*, so it can get away with it). A TeachText document lacks a horizontal scroll bar, because its text never extends beyond the right edge of the window. All of this behavior is a part of TeachText—other programs are free to do things differently (and they do).

Figure 11.14
Resizing the window with text in it—not how most word processors behave.

Closing the Document

1. Click the close box in the upper left corner of the window.

2. Read the dialog box shown in figure 11.15 carefully, thinking through what results from a click of each button.

3. Click the Don't Save button, because we will create a document in the next encounter.

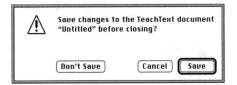

> ⚠ **Save changes to the TeachText document "Untitled" before closing?**
>
> [Don't Save]   [Cancel]   [**Save**]

Figure 11.15
A chance to avert lost data after clicking a document's close box.

Summary

We've finally seen what it's like to begin working inside a program, where we perform our real work. Document windows are where all the action takes place, even if there are some ancillary palettes or tool bars on the screen. If we get by the scary part of doing some work in a window, we've learned that the Mac warns us to save our work before it allows us to close the window.

Exorcises

1. What determines whether a program can have more than one document window open at a time?

2. When multiple windows are allowed, how many can you have open at one time?

3. What distinguishes a document window from other kinds of Macintosh screen windows?

4. A friend asks your help getting started with the new program you don't recognize on the screen. What would you do to find out what the program does and how you start using it?

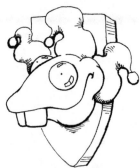

12th Encounter

Storing Your Work

Goal

Master the methods of saving a document in the folder of your choice so that you can organize documents while you work on them.

What You Will Need

The Macintosh turned on and TeachText open with the document window closed (as we left it at the end of the 11th Encounter).

Terms of Enfearment

Save As	default
Save	button
Save File dialog	field
pop-up menu	backup

Briefing

Filing Stuff Away

In the real world, when you finish working with a document, you usually need to put it back into the folder and filing cabinet for safekeeping. Leaving it on your desk makes it vulnerable to being lost or accidentally destroyed in a spilled coffee catastrophe. The same is true for computer documents, but the need to put them away safely is magnified, because unlike the real world, a power outage can wipe out your last hour's work instead of just leaving you in the dark.

Storing documents to the hard disk is called *saving* a document. The longer you have a document open in a program and the more changes you make to it, the more important it becomes to save that document periodically. Saving is a way to put away a snapshot of a document at any given moment—not just when you're finished with it.

Storage Commands

Except for the handful of programs that automatically save changes as we make them (like the Finder does when we rename a folder), all programs have both *Save As* and *Save* commands in their File menus.

Save As...

I discuss the Save As command first, because it's the one we must issue the first time we store a document (if the program lets us choose Save for a new document, it actually reacts as if we had chosen the Save As command anyway). This command leads us to the *Save File dialog* box, a feature-filled window if there ever was one.

In addition to letting us assign a name to the document (an absolute requirement for any document), the Save File dialog also lets us determine exactly where on the hard disk the document should be stored. This is important, because it lets us keep our documents and hard disk organized while we work on the document—we don't have to go out to the Finder to move stuff around. Figure 12.2 shows a generic Save File dialog. Many programs modify this dialog, but the basic elements are always there, even if in a slightly different layout.

Figure 12.1
Choosing Save As... to assign a name and location for a document.

Pop-up menu

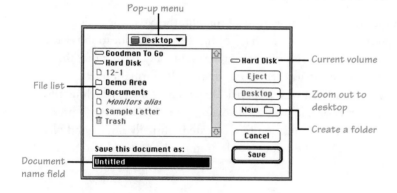

Figure 12.2
The Save File dialog is where we name and store a new document.

Where Are We?

Whenever you see a Save File dialog, it's important to determine which volume and folder the Macintosh is currently pointing to. At a glance, we can see the name of the currently selected volume (hard disk, floppy diskette, file server, etc.), because its name appears above the buttons along the right side of the dialog.

But to see more precisely, we have to check the *pop-up menu* that heads the list of files along the left side of the dialog. Without clicking on anything, we see the name of the folder whose contents are listed in the file list. If we're not sure where this folder is in relation to everything else, we can pull down the pop-up menu (see fig. 12.3). There, we see the series of volume and folders leading from the Desktop to the topmost item on the list. In other words, the list shows us the sequence of disks and folders we would have to open manually in the Finder to reach the currently selected folder.

Figure 12.3
The pop-up menu shows which folder level is currently selected, as well as the path through the folders back to the Desktop.

It's Default of De Program

The first time we save a document in a program, the Save File dialog suggests a place for us to store the file (see fig. 12.4). This location is called the *default*—a common computer term referring to any setting that the computer selects without any help from the user. Performa model Macintoshes are equipped with a special Documents folder, which usually appears as the first choice in a Save File dialog. Other Macs tend to preselect the folder in which the application file is located—usually not a good place to store documents, based on our organization methods described in the 8th Encounter.

Figure 12.4
The first Save As command displays a default location, which may be the folder where the application is or a special Documents folder.

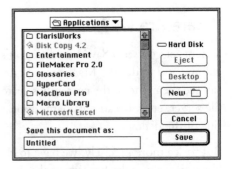

After we save a document to any folder on the hard disk, the next time we see the Save File dialog before quitting the program, it will probably point to the folder of our last save.

Navigating Hard Disk Waters

When it's time to store a document in some place other than the default folder, we use the facilities of the Save File dialog to find our way.

The best way to get used to the place is to jump out to the Desktop level and start our way back in. A convenient Desktop *button* zips us there, or we can choose Desktop from the pop-up menu (see fig. 12.5). In the file list are all items on the Desktop. Only those items that can be opened (disk or file server volumes) are active. From here, we can double-click our way along the path we would normally take in the Finder, opening the disk volume and folder(s) until the folder in which we want to store the document appears in the pop-up menu (see fig. 12.6). Files in the file list appear dimmed, but we can read them to see what else is stored in any given folder from inside this dialog.

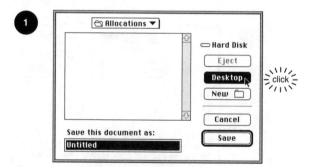

Figure 12.5

Clicking the Desktop button in the Save File dialog takes us to the same items we see when viewing the Desktop on the screen.

Figure 12.6
Upon reaching the
Documents folder.

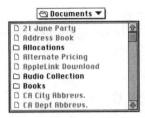

A New Folder button even appears in the dialog, allowing us to create a folder without switching to the Finder (see fig. 12.7).

Figure 12.7
Creating a folder
(Boats) causes that
folder to be nested in
the current folder.

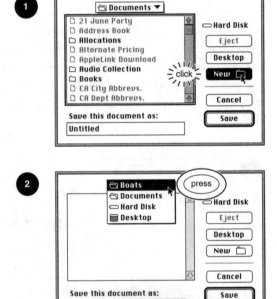

To name the document, it is easiest to press the Tab key until the untitled document name is highlighted in the name *field*. Then type the new name. The Save button has a heavy, highlighted border around it, meaning that a press of the Return or Enter key acts the same as clicking the button (see fig. 12.8).

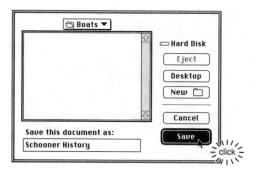

Figure 12.8
The Save button has a heavy outline around it: we can press the Return key to perform the same action as a click.

As you gain experience with Save File dialogs and gain comfort with your document organization, you'll learn that you can navigate more quickly via the pop-up menu. You won't have to go all the way out to the Desktop to wind your way from one folder to another down a completely different path.

Subsequent Saves

After a document is saved on the hard disk, it's much easier to save later revisions. The Save command (and its universal Command-S keyboard equivalent) replaces the old copy with whatever state the document is in at the moment, no matter where on the hard disk the old copy came from (see figs. 12.9 and 12.10). To prevent lost work due to power outages, system crashes, tornadoes and floods, press Command-S every time you reach a point at which you don't want to lose the work you've just performed.

Figure 12.9
Choosing Save periodically is a good precaution against lost data due to power outages or computer problems.

Figure 12.10
Command-S is the keyboard equivalent of the Save command.

Additional Save As Uses

The Save As command comes in handy even after a document is safely stored on the disk. For example, if we want to save each revision of a document, we can't use the Save command over and over, because this command writes over any old version. When we're ready to save a new version, we issue the Save As command and give the document a slightly different name (perhaps append the date).

Saving a second copy of a document is another use for Save As. An extra copy of a file is called a *backup* and can be opened in case the original file is damaged (see fig. 12.11). It is best to save a backup copy to a different volume, because severe data-losing problems tend to affect an entire volume. If another hard disk or file server is on the Desktop, issue the Save As command, zoom out to the Desktop level, choose the desired volume (and nested folder), and save the copy. Most programs provide the name of the file plus the word "copy" as a default name for subsequent Save As commands.

Figure 12.11
Use Save As to save a copy of a file as a backup or as a copy with a different name.

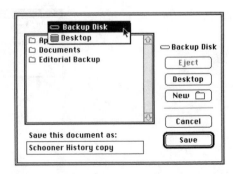

Different from DOS

Few DOS programs have the same commands for saving their documents; whereas the Macintosh is consistent across the field. Macintosh document names can be up to 32 characters long (no colons, however), instead of the DOS 8-dot-3 name limits. The Save File dialog takes care of pathname specifications as you navigate your way through folders with the mouse.

They're Out To Get Us

One of the biggest confusions for new Macintosh users is losing files—not eternally lost, just in some unknown place on the hard disk. If you forget to specify the location in a Save File dialog box, you can always use the Finder's Find command to locate a file by name, date, or kind.

If you feel you're getting lost while navigating through folders via the Save File pop-up menu, press the Desktop button and take it from the top.

Even from the Save File dialog, the Macintosh won't let you overwrite an existing file with the same name within a folder. An alert asks that you confirm your desire to replace an old file with that name (see fig. 12.12). If the old file wasn't created with the same kind of program, another alert may tell you that the replacement wasn't possible. You'll have to find another name or manually trash the older file.

Figure 12.12
You can't accidentally write over an existing file from the Save File dialog without receiving a warning.

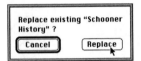

Finally, although the Mac warns you about anything that will lose information, it can't save you from yourself. Closing a changed window without saving the document (clicking "Don't Save") will lose those changes forever. Welcome to personal computing.

Practice

Saving a Document the First Time

1. While in TeachText, choose New from the File menu.

2. Type the memo shown in figure 12.13.

3. Choose Save As.

4. Type the name of the document as *Vacation Memo*, **but don't press Return or Enter yet.**

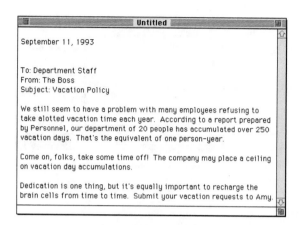

September 11, 1993

To: Department Staff
From: The Boss
Subject: Vacation Policy

We still seem to have a problem with many employees refusing to take alotted vacation time each year. According to a report prepared by Personnel, our department of 20 people has accumulated over 250 vacation days. That's the equivalent of one person-year.

Come on, folks, take some time off! The company may place a ceiling on vacation day accumulations.

Dedication is one thing, but it's equally important to recharge the brain cells from time to time. Submit your vacation requests to Amy.

Figure 12.13
A sample memo that we'll use a lot.

5. Change the current folder to the Documents folder by doing the following:

   a. Clicking the Desktop button.

   b. Double-clicking your hard disk in the file list.

   c. Double-clicking the Documents folder in the file list.

6. Click the New Folder button and create a folder called "Vacation Memo" (see fig. 12.14). Notice that the new folder goes inside the folder previously set as the active folder.

Figure 12.14
Click the New Folder button.

7. Click the Save button (see fig. 12.15). This stores the file on the hard disk.

Figure 12.15
*Click the Save
button.*

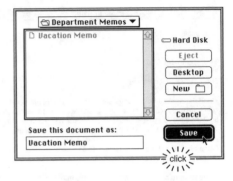

Look for File

1. Switch to the Finder.

2. Choose Find from the File menu, type "Vacation Memo," and press
   Return. The Finder should locate your new file in your new folder.

Subsequent Save

1. Switch back to TeachText.

2. Pull down the File menu. Notice that the Save command is dimmed,
   because there have been no changes since the last save (see fig. 12.16).

Figure 12.16
*With no changes to
save, the Save menu
item is dimmed.*

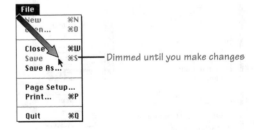

3. Add a few characters to the last paragraph of the document.

4. Pull down the File menu and notice that Save is now active.

5. Type Command-S to issue the Save command (get used to this keyboard combination).

Saving a Backup

1. Choose Save As from the File menu. Notice that the default settings still point to the Department Memos folder.

2. Enter *Vacation Memo Backup* as the file name, **but don't press Return or Enter yet.**

3. Click the Desktop button.

4. Click the Save button to save this backup copy to the Desktop.

5. Notice that the name of the document window has changed to the backup (see fig. 12.17). Choose Save As and see, too, that the default settings point to the Desktop—the last place the document was saved.

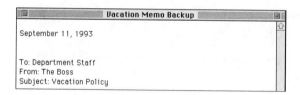

Figure 12.17
After you perform a Save As, the document window has changed to the new title. The original file is still intact.

6. Click the Cancel button.

Summary

For most programs, we must specifically save our work in progress to the hard disk for it to be safe. The Save File dialog lets us give a new document its name and navigate to a location on the hard disk for us to save the document. Save As lets us name and locate a document, and the plain Save command updates the existing file with a copy of our work at the moment.

We should issue the Save command (simplified from the keyboard by Command-S) each time we want to preserve the latest effort that went into a document.

Exorcises

1. In which menu are commands for saving files?

2. Explain the differences between the actions of the Save and Save As commands.

3. You can store documents on the Desktop: True or False?

4. What is a better way of making a backup copy of a document than via the Save As dialog, and why is it better?

5. If you pull down the File menu and the Save item is dimmed, what does that mean?

6. If you choose Save while viewing an untitled, unsaved document, what will happen on the screen?

7. How often should you save a document while you're working on it?

13th Encounter

Quitting and Restarting a Program

Goal

Learn how to quit and restart a program in your sleep.

What You Will Need

Macintosh turned on, TeachText running, and the document created in the 12th Encounter open.

Terms of Enfearment

quit
Restart
force quit
Reset

Briefing

Why Are We Quitting?

There are two reasons why we would want to close down—*quit*—a program:

- We're about to shut down the Macintosh.
- We need to make memory available to load another program.

Before shutting down our Macintosh, we must close down all programs that are running (except for the Finder, which always runs while the Macintosh is on). In fact, if you try shutting down the Macintosh from the Special menu, the Macintosh commands all programs to quit first.

If your machine is running low on available RAM, quitting a program also makes memory available for starting other programs (usually, that is—see the 21st Encounter).

Quit It!

In the File menu of all programs and most desk accessories is the Quit command. Universally, the keyboard Command key equivalent is Command-Q (see fig. 13.1). As we saw earlier, a desk accessory, which tends to appear in a self-contained window, can also be closed down by closing its window. In applications, however, you can close all document windows, and the program still runs.

When we quit a program that has open document windows, the program first checks whether any of those documents need saving because changes have been made to the documents. If so, we see the same dialog box that we get when closing a window of a changed document. It lets us save or discard the changes. This dialog appears for each document that might need saving.

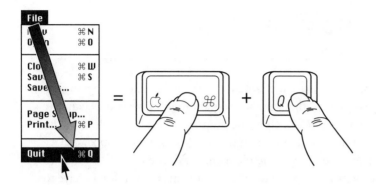

Figure 13.1
*Choosing Quit is
more commonly
performed by typing
Command-Q.*

Restarting a Program

We saw a couple ways to start an application in the 10th Encounter. Those methods apply here to get an application running again, but there is also one nifty speedcut.

A Macintosh document is smart enough to know what application created it. That's why document icons resemble the icons of the programs that created the files. When we double-click on a document icon, the Macintosh immediately starts the program and then loads the document into the program—all ready for us to go (see fig. 13.2). Moreover, if we want to have multiple documents open at the same time (and the program allows it), we can select multiple document icons in the Finder and choose Open from the File menu (see fig. 13.3).

Figure 13.2
*Double-clicking a
document icon also
launches the
program.*

Different from DOS

Few DOS programs offer the same way to quit (or exit) a program, nor is there consistency in the way the program might give you a chance to save a changed document before the program quits. DOS files have no link to the application that created them. Most programs append a three-character extension to the file name (after the period) as a way to help you recognize one program's files from another's, but you have to remember which program generates what extension and how to start the program before you can look at those files.

Figure 13.3
We can also select multiple documents and launch the program by choosing Open from the Finder's File menu.

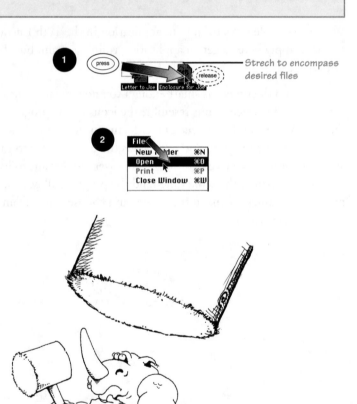

They're Out To Get Us

Sometimes, for no apparent reason (but for probable reasons outlined in the 20th Encounter), a program may freeze up on you—the pointer may react to the mouse, but nothing you click on does anything. A *freeze* is also known as a *hang*, which is usually what you want to do to yourself if you haven't saved your work recently. When this happens, try the following steps in order:

1. Type Command-period. Some programs might be in an endless loop, which this keyboard command can break.

2. Press the Escape key. It can't hurt.

3. Hold down the Command, Option, and Escape keys (see fig. 13.4). You'll get the *Force Quit* dialog shown in figure 13.5, which lets you quit the current program without disturbing others that are running (and may have unsaved work open). Click the Force Quit button. If nothing happens, proceed to step 4; otherwise, save all the work in other applications, quit them, and restart your Mac by choosing Restart in the Finder's Special menu.

Figure 13.4
Pressing Command-Option-Escape results in the Force Quit dialog.

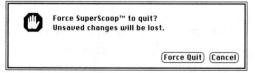

Figure 13.5
The Force Quit dialog.

4. Look for a front, side, or rear panel push-button that looks like a key with a left-pointing triangle and press it. Not all Mac models have this *Reset* button readily available. If yours does, and you press it, the machine should restart. If it still doesn't, go to the last step.

5. Turn off the Macintosh via the power button or switch on the back of the machine. This is the last resort but will certainly get you out of a jam.

Although opening an application by double-clicking one of its documents is neat, it may not work if the application that created the file is not on your hard disk (see fig. 13.6). This can easily happen if someone gives you a file from another machine that contains other types of programs. If you know what kind of file it is (e.g., word processing, graphics), you may be able to open the file from within a similar kind of application. Many programs can open and convert files from other formats.

Figure 13.6

Someone might give us a document file created by software we don't have installed in our Mac.

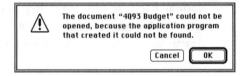

Practice

Quitting

1. Add a few words to the open Vacation Memo document in TeachText. We'll discard these changes later.

2. Pull down the File menu and notice the Quit command—but do not choose it now.

3. Open the Calculator desk accessory if it isn't already open; otherwise choose it from the Application menu to make it the active program.

4. View—but don't choose—the Quit command in the File menu.

5. Open the Note Pad desk accessory.

6. Choose Quit from the File menu. Notice how the program zooms back to the Desktop.

7. Choose Quit from the File menu. The Calculator zooms back to the Desktop.

8. Type Command-Q. Read the fail-safe dialog about the Vacation Memo document (see fig. 13.7).

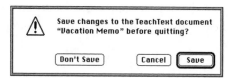

Figure 13.7
Know what each of the button choices means.

9. Click Cancel to bring you back to the state just prior to issuing the Quit command.

10. Type Command-Q again and click the Don't Save button.

Restarting a Program

1. In the Finder, locate the original Vacation Memo file.

2. Select the icon and choose Get Info from the File menu. Notice how the file knows it came from TeachText (see fig. 13.8). Close the Get Info window.

```
┌──────────────────────────────┐
│ ▦▦ Vacation Memo Info ▦▦▦    │
├──────────────────────────────┤
│  ▤  Vacation Memo            │
│                              │
│  Kind: TeachText document    │
│  Size: 6K on disk (582 bytes used) │
│                              │
│  Where: Hard Disk : Documents : │
│                              │
│  Created: Tue, Feb 2, 1993, 12:03 AM │
│  Modified: Tue, Feb 2, 1993, 12:03 AM │
│  Version: n/a                │
│  Comments:                   │
│  ┌────────────────────────┐  │
│  │                        │  │
│  │                        │  │
│  └────────────────────────┘  │
│  □ Locked      □ Stationery pad │
└──────────────────────────────┘
```

A document knows whence it came

Figure 13.8
The document knows it came from TeachText.

3. Double-click the Vacation Memo file icon.

4. Type Command-Q to quit the program. There were no changes to the document, so you're not asked to save any.

Summary

We've learned the universal way to quit any Macintosh application. Documents know which applications created them, so we can re-open a document and its application by just double-clicking the document icon in the Finder.

Exorcises

1. Where do you look for the Quit command in Macintosh applications?

2. In the dialog in figure 13.9, describe the results of clicking each of the buttons.

Figure 13.9
*What happens when
you click each
button?*

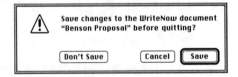

14th Encounter

Working with an Existing Document

Goal

Start using basic text-editing techniques, while learning how to shuffle text and pictures from document to document or program to program.

What You Will Need

Macintosh turned on, with all applications and desk accessories closed.

Terms of Enfearment

Open File dialog	Cut
text insertion pointer	Paste
text cursor	Undo
font	Scrapbook
Clipboard	draw objects
Copy	bit maps

Briefing

Opening a Document

We've already learned how to open a document from the Finder by double-clicking it. But when we're already inside a program, we can open a document without switching to the Finder. All document-oriented programs provide an Open command in the File menu (see fig. 14.1).

Figure 14.1
Choosing Open in an application's File menu is one way to open an existing document file.

This ellipsis-toting command leads to an *Open File dialog* box, a simpler cousin of the Save File dialog we've already met. In fact, because we know how to use the Save File, we already know everything there is to know about the Open File dialog: how to navigate through volumes and folders to locate a file (see fig. 14.2). The only difference in behavior is that file names are not dimmed in the file list. To open a file, we select it and click the Open button—or better yet, double-click on the file name.

Figure 14.2
We navigate our way through folders in the Open File dialog box to locate a document of our choice.

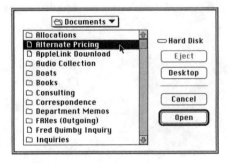

Don't freak out if you don't see every file you know to be in a given folder. Programs tend to filter out those files that it cannot open while preparing items for the file list.

Typing Text

Unless your work is entirely graphical, a lot of what you do on the Macintosh is entering and editing text in documents. We had a taste of this in creating the vacation memo in the 12th Encounter. As we typed, the *text insertion pointer*—the flashing vertical line in document—pointed to where the next character we typed would go. This insertion pointer is independent of the mouse pointer.

Positioning the Pointer

We do, however, use the mouse pointer to re-position the text insertion pointer within a chunk of text. Whenever the mouse pointer rolls atop an editable area, the pointer changes its appearance from the arrow to a *text cursor.* The text cursor is one pixel wide for a reason: it lets us position it *between* characters in a line of text. If we then click the mouse button, the flashing text insertion pointer appears in that spot. The next characters we type insert themselves starting at that location, pushing the text after it to the right and down. Macintosh text never overwrites other text (unless that other text is selected).

Short Moves

If we need to move the text insertion pointer only a few characters or lines, it may be more convenient to use the four cursor keys on the keyboard (see fig. 14.3). A press of each of these keys moves the text insertion pointer one unit (character or line) in the direction of the arrow. Some programs enhance this motion if we hold down a modifier key, such as the Command key, to do things like jump forward or back by a full word, rather than by one character.

Figure 14.3
*Keyboard
cursor keys.*

Extended
keyboard

Apple and
PowerBook
keyboards

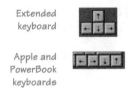

Selecting Text

Much of Macintosh operation consists of a sequence of the following:

- Selecting something

- Issuing a command that affects the selected item

The same is true for working with text. We must first select a range of characters—from a single character to the entire document, if necessary— and then issue a command.

As shown in figure 14.4, we use the mouse pointer to select text in a three-step series:

1. Position the mouse pointer (in its text cursor shape) to the left of the character where the selection begins.

2. Click and drag the pointer until it is located to the right of the last character of the selection. As we drag, the area becomes highlighted.

3. Release the mouse button.

Figure 14.4
*Click and drag
across text to select it.*

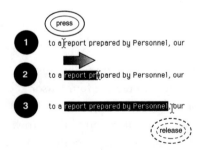

After text is selected, we can make menu choices that affect the selection, such as changing the *font* style to boldface. The selection persists, so we can perform additional actions on the same selection (e.g., increasing the size of the characters). A click anywhere else deselects the text.

Selection Speedcuts

Common to all Macintosh text editing are a couple speedcuts to make work life a bit easier. The most important is a double-click on a word to select the entire word (see fig. 14.5). Text-intensive programs usually have additional, non-standard speedcuts such as this to select entire lines or paragraphs.

Figure 14.5
Double-click anywhere in a word to select the entire word.

Another useful speedcut helps select a large chunk of text even if it extends down several scrollings of a document window (see fig. 14.6). The steps are as follows:

1. Position the text insertion pointer at the beginning of the intended selection.

2. If necessary, *without clicking in the document*, scroll down until the end of the selection is in view.

3. Hold down the Shift key and click at the end of the intended selection.

①
> We still seem to have a problem with many employees refusing to take alotted vacation time each year. According to a report prepared by Personnel, our department of 20 people has accumulated over 250 vacation days. That's the equivalent of one person-year.

②
> We still seem to have a problem with many employees refusing to take alotted vacation time each year. According to a report prepared by Personnel, our department of 20 people has accumulated over 250 vacation days. That's the equivalent of one person-year.

Figure 14.6
Click once at the beginning and Shift-click to select an entire region, even if you must scroll to reach the bottom.

The entire range is instantly selected, and any action we perform works on the entire range, even if not all of it is in view.

Moving Text Around

Built into the Macintosh is a most convenient facility called the *Clipboard*— a temporary storage space for anything we can select in a document. When something is stored in the Clipboard, we can take it to another place in the document, to another document, and even to another program.

To get something into the Clipboard, we first select it. Then we issue one of two commands in the Edit menu: *Copy* or *Cut*. Copy places an exact copy of the selected information into the Clipboard, leaving the original intact (see fig. 14.7); Cut, on the other hand, removes the original after copying it to the Clipboard (see fig. 14.8).

Figure 14.7
Copying places the selected information into a special place in memory called the Clipboard.

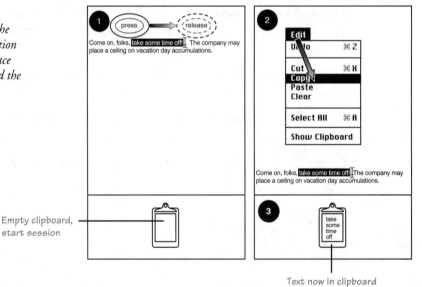

Empty clipboard, start session

Text now in clipboard

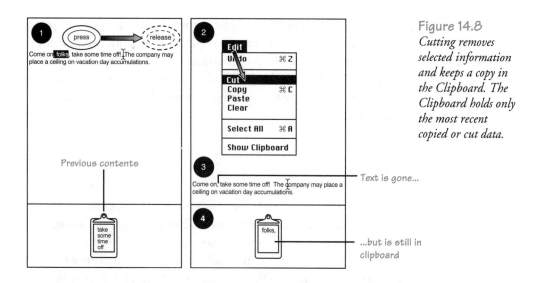

Figure 14.8
*Cutting removes
selected information
and keeps a copy in
the Clipboard. The
Clipboard holds only
the most recent
copied or cut data.*

To get something out of the Clipboard and into a document, we issue the
Paste command. To paste text, however, we must first indicate where we
want it to go by positioning the flashing text insertion pointer at the desired
location. The Paste command then inserts the data from the Clipboard into
the document (see fig. 14.9).

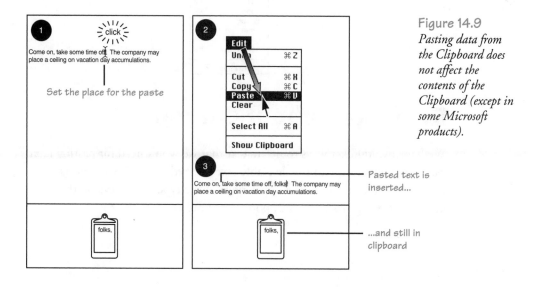

Figure 14.9
*Pasting data from
the Clipboard does
not affect the
contents of the
Clipboard (except in
some Microsoft
products).*

Pasting information does not remove it from the Clipboard, so we can paste the same Clipboard information in as many places as we want. Because the Clipboard can hold only one piece of information at a time, however, the next time we Copy or Cut anything, we will overwrite what was in there before. Most importantly, the Clipboard is also wiped clean when the Macintosh switches off.

OH NO!

Just like working with scissors and glue, it is possible while cutting and pasting on the Macintosh to cut the wrong stuff or paste it in the wrong place. This is where the Mac has one up over the real world. As long as we recognize an error right away, we can usually make everything better by choosing the *Undo* command in the Edit menu (see fig. 14.10). Not all programs offer Undo (TeachText doesn't for example), but most do. Issuing the Undo command after an errant Cut restores the text to its uncut state; after an errant Paste, Undo lifts the inserted text from the document.

Figure 14.10
The Undo command can often recover from a mistake.

Deleting without Cutting

We have two quicker ways to delete text that we won't need for pasting later. Both methods start with the deletable text selected. One is as simple as pressing the Delete key at the upper right of the typewriter keys on the keyboard (see fig. 14.11). Press, poof: it's gone.

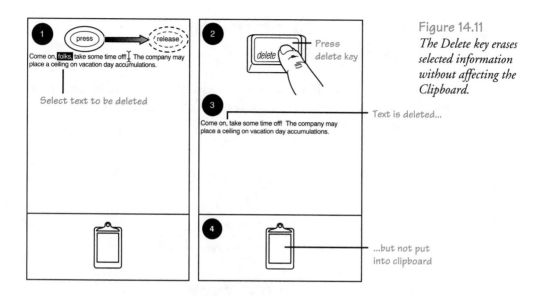

Figure 14.11
The Delete key erases selected information without affecting the Clipboard.

When the deleted text is actually going to be replaced by text we type or by text pasted from the Clipboard, all we have to do is select the deletable text. The next character we type or chunk we paste removes the selected text (see fig. 14.12). Well-designed programs make even these deleting actions undoable. Thank Heaven for Undo!

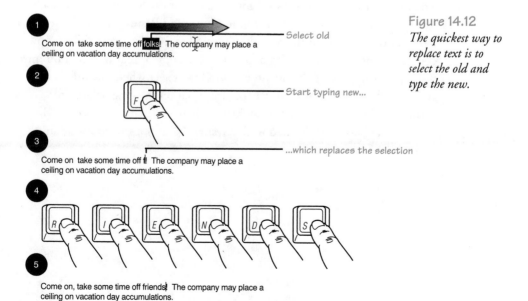

Figure 14.12
The quickest way to replace text is to select the old and type the new.

Long-Term Clipboard: The Scrapbook

Because the Clipboard is wiped clean when we shut down the Macintosh, it is not the best place to store frequently used tidbits—chunks of favorite text, art, and sounds. But, the *Scrapbook* desk accessory fills the gap (see fig. 14.13).

Figure 14.13
Opening the Scrapbook.

The Scrapbook automatically stores on disk whatever bits and pieces we like—anything the Clipboard can hold. Moreover, we can open the Scrapbook from within an application and transfer information to or from a Scrapbook page.

The mechanism for shifting stuff into and out of the Scrapbook is actually the Clipboard in concert with the Cut, Copy, and Paste commands (see fig. 14.14). For example, in the Scrapbook, scroll to a desired page. The Copy command applies to the entire page, placing a copy of that information into the clipboard. Activate the document window, select where the info is to go, and issue the Paste command. Pasting information into the Scrapbook automatically creates a new page, which is then automatically saved to disk (in the Scrapbook File, located in the System Folder) for us to use at any time in the future.

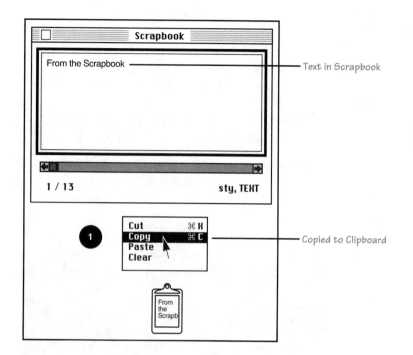

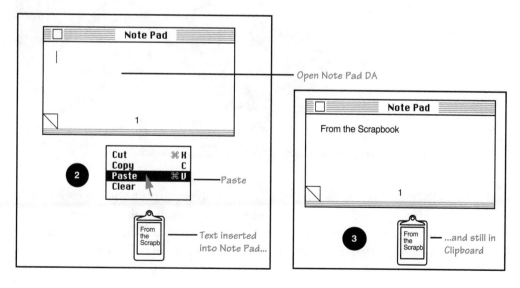

Figure 14.14
To transfer information into or out of the Scrapbook, we actually use the Clipboard's facilities for copying and pasting.

Selecting Graphics

While we're talking about selecting, copying, and pasting stuff, I'll just touch on how to work with graphics documents. The trick is knowing how to select graphics, which depends on whether the graphics are objects (somewhat tangible items, often called *draw objects*) or just collections of pixels in the document (usually called *bit maps*—a layout of pixels).

Graphics objects let us click on them as distinct elements of the document. A selected object displays four or more rectangles at the corners (see fig. 14.15). Such objects can be dragged, copied, or cut. These are the easiest kinds of graphics to work with.

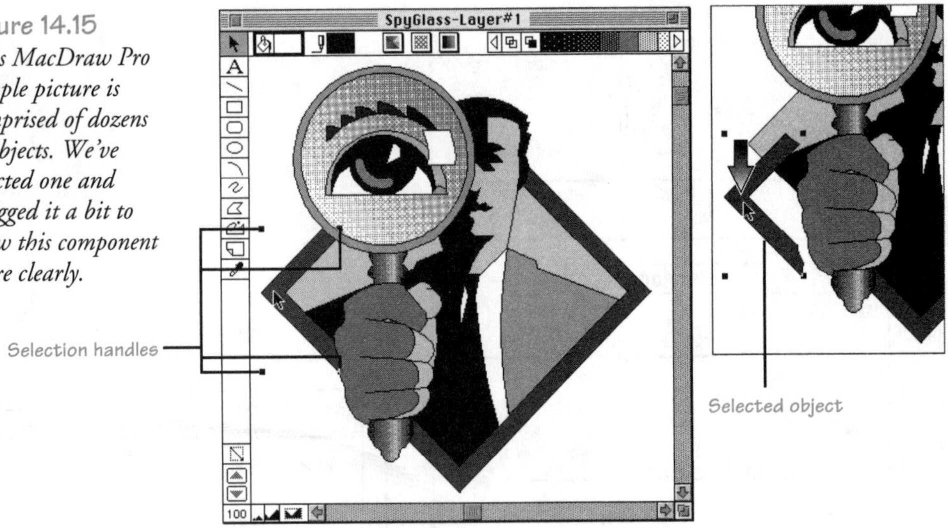

Figure 14.15
This MacDraw Pro sample picture is comprised of dozens of objects. We've selected one and dragged it a bit to show this component more clearly.

Selection handles

Selected object

Selecting bit maps is a bit trickier. It usually requires one of two tools found in the program's tools palette (see fig. 14.16). Both tools let us draw an area on the screen to select, either in a freehand outline we draw (lasso tool) or in a rectangle (selection rectangle tool). After we make a selection, the outline of the area or every dark pixel within the area flickers. Specific behavior of such a selection varies from program to program, but that's one way to get art into the Scrapbook for insertion into other documents.

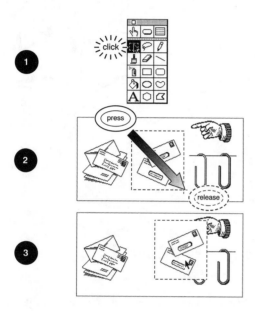

Figure 14.16
Here, we use HyperCard's selection rectangle to select a region of pixels and then drag that region to the right.

Different from DOS

A lot of text programs in DOS offer you the choice of insert or typeover modes, but the Mac is always in insert mode. Also, depending on the software, the equivalent of the text insertion pointer is often a highlighted character, rather than a position clearly between characters. Other inconsistencies among programs—selecting text for subsequent actions, moving chunks, and deleting—make for a lot of remembering how each program does what.

They're Out To Get Us

Be angry, but don't be surprised if some egregious error you want undone doesn't undo. First of all, you usually have to catch your error right away before doing anything else that is undo-able, because programs generally remember only the last undo-able thing they do. Also, sometimes programs don't support undo for every action. It never hurts to try Undo, but it will hurt when it doesn't work when you need it.

Microsoft products do some Clipboard things differently than other programs. Cutting, copying, and pasting in Excel, for example, uses a one-shot Clipboard, which clears itself after one paste. Also, sometimes you'll see an alert asking whether you want to preserve the contents of a large clipboard before switching to another program. What this is really asking you is whether it should bother converting its internal clipboard to the generic Mac Clipboard so that you can use the data in another program. A smaller clipboard automatically converts when switching out of the program.

One last important gotcha here is that not all documents can accept all types of information from the Clipboard or Scrapbook. TeachText documents, for example, do not accept graphics pasted from the Clipboard. The Paste command doesn't do anything when you try pasting a graphic. Programs try their best to use what they can from the Clipboard, but sometimes it's a case of comparing kiwis to kumquats.

Practice

Opening a File

1. Activate TeachText and choose Open from the File menu.

2. Locate the Vacation Memo file and double-click its entry in the file list (see fig. 14.17).

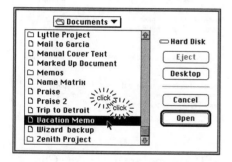

Figure 14.17
Locate "Vacation Memo."

Entering and Replacing Text

1. Position the text insertion pointer between the words *a* and *problem* in the first line of the first paragraph of the body of the memo.

2. Type "serious" and a space to add the word (see fig. 14.18).

We still seem to have a serious problem

Figure 14.18
Add a word to the first line.

3. Double-click the word to select it.

4. Type "major" to replace the selected word.

Moving Text to Another Program

1. Select the To, From, and Subject lines only through the colon following "Subject" (see fig. 14.19).

Figure 14.19
*Drag-select the lines
shown.*

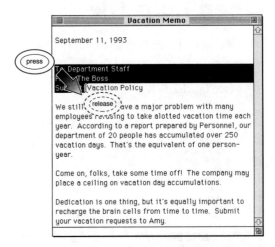

2. Choose Copy from the Edit menu. Those lines are now in the Clipboard.

3. Choose Show Clipboard from the Edit menu to prove it.

4. Switch to the Finder.

5. Choose Show Clipboard from the Edit menu. The contents of the Clipboard survives switching between applications (see fig. 14.20).

Figure 14.20
The Finder Clipboard window shows that the contents are still there after switching to the Finder.

6. Open the Note Pad desk accessory from the Apple menu.

7. Choose Paste from the Edit menu. A copy of those lines are now in the Note Pad (see fig. 14.21).

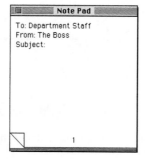

Figure 14.21
Pasting the Clipboard's contents into the Note Pad.

Playing with Undo

1. Insert the word "Date:" and today's date above the text (press Return at the end of the line to shift the other lines down).

2. Choose Undo from the Edit menu. The Note Pad supports undo for typed text, so your last text entry is undone.

3. Press Command-Z (Undo) a few times to toggle between the two versions.

4. Select all the text in this Note Pad page and press the Delete key to remove it.

5. Close the Note Pad window.

The Scrapbook

1. Open the Scrapbook via the Apple menu.

2. Choose Paste from the Edit menu. The lines of text from our previous copy go into a new page of the Scrapbook (see fig. 14.22).

Figure 14.22

Pasting again, this time into the Scrapbook.

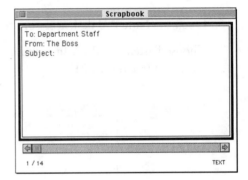

3. Scroll the Scrapbook until you see the world map graphic.

4. Choose Copy from the Edit menu. This replaces the Clipboard contents with the map.

5. Activate TeachText.

6. Choose Show Clipboard from the Edit menu. You see the map in figure 14.23.

Figure 14.23

The map is in TeachText's Clipboard, but the program cannot accept graphic data by pasting it in.

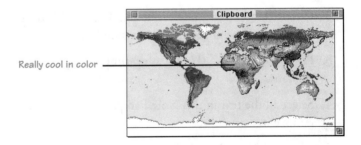

7. Choose Paste from the Edit menu. Nothing happens, because TeachText doesn't accept pasted graphics.

The Ephemeral Clipboard

1. Quit all programs.

2. Choose Show Clipboard from the Edit menu. The map is still in there.

3. Choose Restart from the Special menu. This action erases the Clipboard without asking or reminding.

4. When the Mac is back up, choose Show Clipboard from the Edit menu. It is empty upon startup.

Cut, Copy, Paste from Keyboard

1. Open the Scrapbook and bring the Vacation Memo text lines into view.

2. Type Command-X (Cut) to clear that page of the Scrapbook while putting the text into the Clipboard.

3. Start TeachText.

4. In a blank, untitled window, type Command-V (Paste).

5. Place the text insertion pointer anywhere in the text and type Command-V again.

6. Spend several minutes cutting, copying, and pasting sections of text using the skills of selecting and issuing commands from the keyboard (Command-X, -C, and -V).

Summary

In this action-packed encounter, we've seen how to open existing documents and how to use basic text-editing skills. The Clipboard and, to a lesser extent, the Scrapbook are important facilities to aid in working with documents and their contents.

Exorcises

1. Describe the primary differences between the Scrapbook and Clipboard.

2. What are all the ways to get information into the Clipboard?

3. What are all the ways to get information out of the Clipboard into a document?

4. What is the most efficient way to replace existing text with something new from the keyboard?

5. How would you use the Scrapbook without the Clipboard?

6. Describe the steps you would use to move an entire paragraph from one location in a document to another location in the same document.

15th Encounter

Printing a Document

Goal

To learn how to navigate through the dialog boxes required to print a document.

What You Will Need

Macintosh turned on, with TeachText running and the Vacation Memo file open; a printer connected to your Macintosh and its power switched on.

Terms of Enfearment

ImageWriter	zone
StyleWriter	background printing
LaserWriter	spooling
Chooser	Page Setup
printer driver	portrait (vertical) printing
AppleTalk	landscape (sideways) printing

Briefing

Know Thy Printer

Before we can do any printing, it is vital that we know what kind of printer is connected to the Macintosh. Each class of printer expects different signals from the Macintosh, so we have to tell our Mac which printer it will be talking to.

Apple has produced a number of different printers for the Mac over the years. The most popular ones are the *ImageWriter*, *StyleWriter*, and various *LaserWriter* models. As far as the Mac is concerned, most LaserWriters are the same. The exceptions are the LaserWriter IISC, Personal LaserWriter LS, and possibly new inexpensive LaserWriters that Apple may release at any time. It is also possible that your Macintosh is connected to a non-Apple printer. That's fine, provided the printer is compatible with the Mac (and comes with software the Mac needs to communicate with the printer).

You, Over There!

The first step in making your Mac printable is using a desk accessory called the *Chooser* to tell the Mac which printer you're using. As shown in figure 15.1, the Chooser displays icons representing *printer driver* files located in the Extensions Folder (inside the System Folder). Printer drivers are files that contain instructions the Mac uses to control a specific type of printer. If we remember that selecting a driver essentially directs the Mac to print to the selected device, we can also understand how a FAX modem may be considered a printing device, because the Mac must "print" to the FAX modem, where the signals are converted to audio tones for transfer over the telephone.

Open the Chooser

Figure 15.1
The Chooser desk accessory lets us tell our Mac which printer model we have. Here, we include a driver for a non-Apple printer.

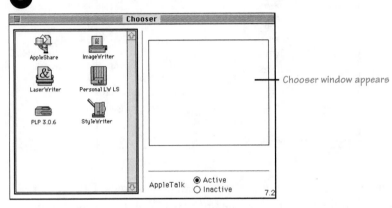

Chooser window appears

After we choose a printer, the Mac remembers the setting, and we don't have to bother with this unless we change printers.

For each printer we select in the Chooser, a set of other settings present themselves in the Chooser.

Chooser Settings, Part I

For ImageWriter and StyleWriter printers, the most important choice is which serial connector (port) the printer is connected to (see fig. 15.2). Two icons, representing the modem and printer ports from the back of the computer, appear in the Chooser. Although we can use either one (unless our Mac has only one serial port), the printer port is more desirable. In any case, just click on the port to which the printer is cabled.

Figure 15.2
Choices on the right for the StyleWriter include the port to which the printer is cabled and the background printing status.

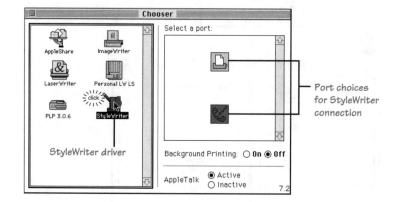

LaserWriter settings can be more complicated, because most LaserWriters are connected to the Mac via an *AppleTalk* network. Actually, most of the networking stuff is built into the Mac and printers, so all it takes to set up a network for a Mac and a printer is the proper cabling. We must also inform the Mac that we intend to print via AppleTalk: the AppleTalk Active button must be selected (and the machine restarted if AppleTalk was previously inactive).

It is also possible that more than one printer is on the network; the network may also be so large that it is divided into more than one *zone*. The Chooser lets you select the zone (if applicable) and printer. All LaserWriter printers have a name assigned by the person who set up the printer in the first place (see fig. 15.3). Printer names help us differentiate one printer from any others that may be on the same network and listed in the Chooser (see fig. 15.4).

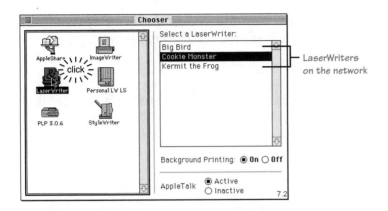

Figure 15.3
LaserWriters have names. More than one LaserWriter may be connected to a network, so you can direct printed output to any one of them via the Chooser.

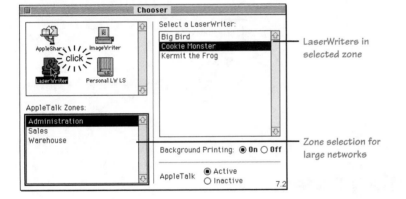

Figure 15.4
More complex networks are divided into subgroups— zones—each of which may have a variety of LaserWriters.

Chooser Settings, Part II

Many printer drivers allow *background printing*. This handy feature lets a program perform its internal printing tasks quickly, while a copy of the printed file is saved to disk. While we work on other stuff, the system software sends the document to the printer page-by-page without us having to wait for the document to reach real paper (although the computer sometimes freezes momentarily while sending signals to the printer). If a background printing radio button, such as the one shown in figure 15.5, is available for a printer, it's a good idea to use it, because it may improve your productivity on the computer. Background printing is also known by the name *spooling*, and the software that monitors spooling is called a *spooler*.

The Mac's spooling software is called PrintMonitor, which we can open from the Application menu only when it is tending to files yet to reach the printer (see fig. 15.6).

Figure 15.5

Turning on Background Printing lets us work on other things as the Mac sends documents to the printer.

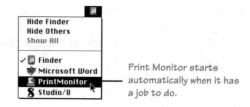

Background Printing: ⦿ **On** ○ **Off**

Figure 15.6

When it kicks in, PrintMonitor handles print spooling for us. Choosing PrintMonitor lets us see how the spooler is doing.

Hide Finder
Hide Others
Show All

✓ 🖥 Finder
🕷 Microsoft Word
📄 PrintMonitor
𝟴 Studio/8

Print Monitor starts
automatically when it has
a job to do.

Printing Sideways

Sometimes documents are wider than a typical page. Spreadsheets and graphics, especially, may be printed best with the paper sideways. All Macintosh printers accommodate this, but the control for it is in a special dialog available in all printable applications. In the File menu, usually immediately above the Print command, is a *Page Setup* command (see fig. 15.7).

Figure 15.7

Each document stores printing attributes set by Page Setup.

File	
New	⌘N
Open...	⌘O
Close	⌘W
Save	⌘S
Save As...	
Page Setup...	
Print...	⌘P
Quit	⌘Q

The Page Setup dialog varies significantly from driver to driver, because each printer model has a specific range of settings. However, they all share in common a two-icon selection between vertical (*portrait*) and sideways (*landscape*) printing (see fig. 15.8). These settings also affect the document in the document window. The virtual page on the screen usually changes so that it is turned sideways. Therefore, it's best to make this setting early in your work on a document. Page Setup affects only the active document and is saved as an attribute of the document in its file. Thus, we can choose an envelope paper size and save it with an envelope file.

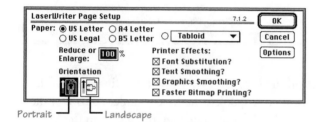

Portrait ──┘   └── Landscape

Figure 15.8
Page Setup dialogs vary from printer to printer, but all let us set the page orientation.

Can We Print Now?

To print a document, make sure that it is the active window in the application and choose Print from the File menu. That's not all, however. A *Print dialog* appears, giving us some further control over the printing (see fig. 15.9). Among the most important optional settings are how many copies we want, if we want just a portion of a document or all pages, and whether the paper will come from the paper tray or from our manually feeding a special kind of paper (or envelope).

Figure 15.9
*Choosing Print in an
application produces
the Print dialog.
Click Print to start
printing.*

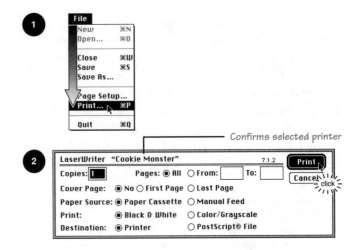

Click the Print button, and the Mac takes over. Until the final page of the
document is sent to the printer or spooler, the Mac is under control of the
application program, preventing us from doing anything else on the Mac.
Now, we can see that spooling makes productive sense.

Different from DOS

Very often, each DOS program requires its own printer driver or
printer setting for your printer, but on the Mac, this is a system-wide
function taking care of all applications. How you issue the printing
command varies widely across DOS programs. Also, not all programs
provide landscape printing facilities.

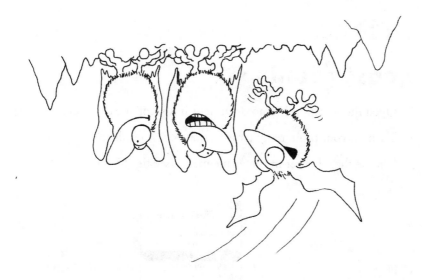

They're Out To Get Us

One of the most disconcerting events to happen in this process of preparing your Mac for printing is opening the Chooser and not finding an icon for your printer model. If you have an Apple printer, you'll have to dig out the system software diskettes and look for the disk containing printer information. On that disk is an installer that lets you elect (via the Custom Install route) to install printer files for your printer. If your printer isn't an Apple printer, it probably came with a diskette containing the proper driver. All drivers go into the Extensions Folder of the System Folder.

Another troubling symptom is to not see the name of the desired LaserWriter in the Chooser. The printer must be turned on for the Chooser to see it. Also, AppleTalk cables running along the floor can loosen by an inadvertent kick, so check that all connections along the cable route are secure.

Printing problems are nightmares, because they usually occur when you're in the biggest rush to get something out. You'll pick up tips along the way from experience, such as printing just one copy of a job to make sure that everything is okay before printing the other 24 copies.

Practice

Chooser Settings

1. Open the Vacation Memo document if it's not already open.

2. Turn on your printer and let it warm up, if it needs to.

3. Choose the Chooser in the Apple menu (see fig. 15.10).

Figure 15.10
Choose the Chooser.

4. Click on the icon of the printer model you have.

5. ImageWriter/StyleWriter users should do the following:

   a. Click on the Printer icon if the printer is cabled to that connector.

   b. Click the Background Printing On button, if available.

   LaserWriter users should do the following:

   a. If your LaserWriter is connected via a network, be sure that the AppleTalk Active button is selected. If not, click on the button and restart your Mac before continuing.

   b. If you are connected to a large network, ask the network administrator for the name of the zone containing the printer you'll be using and select that from the list of zones in the lower left of the Chooser.

   c. Select the name of the LaserWriter you are to use.

6. Close the Chooser to save these settings.

Page Setup

1. Choose Page Setup from the TeachText File menu (see fig. 15.11). Notice the settings available for your printer. We'll use the default settings, as most documents do.

2. Click Cancel.

3. Choose Print from the File menu.

4. Click Print in the Print dialog to use the default settings.

Figure 15.11
Choose Page Setup.

5. Go to the printer and wait for the results.

6. Choose Page Setup from the File menu again, click the landscape icon (see fig. 15.12), and click OK.

Figure 15.12
Click the landscape option.

7. Choose Print from the File menu.

8. Click Print and wait for the document to print in landscape mode.

9. If you want to save this setting with the document, choose Save from the File menu.

10. Quit TeachText (don't save changes if you're asked).

Summary

We've learned that much of the technical wizardry of managing the printer is handled by system software, accessible to us via the Chooser, Page Setup, and Print dialogs. Chooser settings need be made only once to cover all applications and documents, but Page Setup settings are saved as part of each document. Printing subsequent copies or versions involves only the Print command and Print dialog. No matter what, a printer driver for the printer must be in the Extensions Folder.

Exorcises

1. What determines the correct communications between your Macintosh and printer?

2. Detail the steps required to print two copies of pages 5 to 10 of a document.

3. Describe background printing and what it means to your productivity.

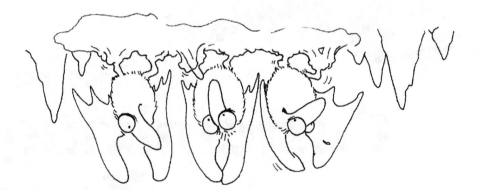

Customizing Your Environment

Goal

Learn how to make important system settings and to simplify application launching.

What You Will Need

Macintosh turned on; today's date; an accurate time signal.

Terms of Enfearment

control panel
beep sound
alias
Apple Menu Items Folder
Startup Items Folder

Briefing

Be in Control

Buried within the System Folder is a collection of files that gives us immense power over the way our Macintosh behaves. These files are known as *control panels* and are located in a folder called, conveniently enough, Control Panels. We can open that folder directly by choosing Control Panels from the Apple menu. Your Control Panels folder may contain many more files than the basic ones shown in figure 16.1.

Figure 16.1
Choosing Control Panels in the Apple menu opens a folder containing our Mac's Control Panels.

Open the Control Panels folder

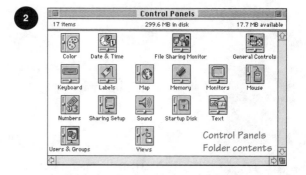

Control Panels Folder contents

Most control panel files have a distinctive slider control in their icons. To access a control panel, double-click its icon.

It's About Time

One important Mac feature we can control by a control panel is the internal clock, which keeps track of the date and time, even when the machine is turned off. It's important to have the clock set correctly, because that's where the modified dates for files come from (see fig. 16.2). You may also use programs that keep your schedule or sound alarms for you—they *must* have access to the current date and time to be of any use.

Figure 16.2
The Mac updates the modification date and time for any file we work with, but the internal clock must be set for these dates to be accurate.

Setting the Time

Although there are a couple of ways to set the clock, we'll show you the General Controls panel (see fig. 16.3). It's not essential to set the clock to the second, but here's how to do it:

1. Click on the hour figure and type the current hour.

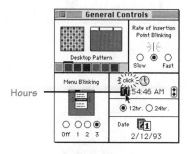

Figure 16.3
Setting the time via the General Controls panel starts with clicking on the hour and typing the current hour. Tab to the minutes setting.

2. Click on or tab to the minutes figure and type the next minute.

3. Click on or tab to the seconds figure and type the figure zero.

4. Click on or tab to the AM or PM and type A or P, whichever it is at the moment.

5. At the sound of the tone for the next minute, click the little clock icon.

Figure 16.4
Set the seconds to zero and click the clock icon to synchronize with a time signal.

Setting the date is just as easy. Click on each segment of the date and enter the appropriate values. Click on the little calendar icon when finished (see fig. 16.5).

Figure 16.5
Set the date digits the same way and click the calendar icon for the changes to take effect.

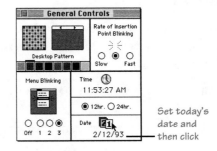

To close any control panel, click the close box at the top left of its window.

Figure 16.6
Close control panels by clicking their windows' close boxes.

Mouse/Pointer Speed

I mentioned in the 4th Encounter that we can set the speed at which the pointer on the screen reacts to quick motion of the mouse. This is done in the Mouse control panel, by adjusting the Tracking Speed (see fig. 16.7). The further to the right our selection, the faster the pointer moves in reaction to faster mouse or trackball motion—allowing us to cover more screen real estate with less desk real estate or ball rolling (see fig. 16.8).

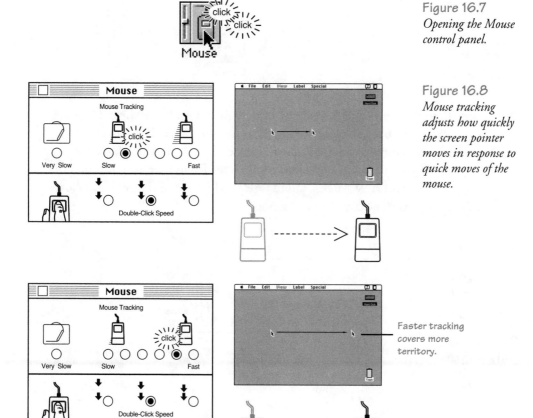

Figure 16.7
Opening the Mouse control panel.

Figure 16.8
Mouse tracking adjusts how quickly the screen pointer moves in response to quick moves of the mouse.

Faster tracking covers more territory.

Beep Beep

In response to various actions, the Macintosh or applications generate an audio clue that something is wrong—like clicking outside a dialog box when the only operations allowed at the moment are those within the dialog. Known as the *beep sound*, the actual sound may be something quite different from a beep. In fact, we can choose the sound we want from a selection supplied with the Macintosh. All this is controlled by the Sound control panel (see fig. 16.9).

Figure 16.9

Opening the Sound control panel.

Both the sound and the volume of the sound are adjusted here. Drag the slider control to any point along the scale and release the mouse button to hear the currently selected sound at the currently selected volume (see fig. 16.10). Click on any sound name in the list to hear what it sounds like (see fig. 16.11). Whatever sound is selected when the control panel closes is the one we'll hear as the beep sound.

Figure 16.10

Drag the volume slider control to adjust the audio level. When you release the mouse button, a sample plays through the speaker at the selected volume.

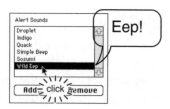

Figure 16.11
*Click on each sound
to hear what it
sounds like. Close the
control panel to
make the selected
sound your Mac's
beep sound.*

If your Macintosh comes with a microphone, you can even record extra
sounds to add to the list. But, this would be like having fun—and we're
supposed to be doing our work.

Built-in Screen Brightness

Although we may be used to adjusting video screen brightness by fiddling
with a knob, such is not the case with recent Macs that have built-in black-
and-white monitors. A Brightness control panel lets you adjust a slider (like
the audio volume control) for the most comfortable brightness level.

Filling Up the Apple Menu

Earlier I said there is a way to place our applications into the Apple menu to
make them easy to launch without opening a bunch of folders to find them.
But, we also want to do this so that the neat organization of our folders and
applications is not upset. For this, we call upon a helpful Macintosh feature
called the *alias.*

A.K.A.

Imagine a childhood friend whose real name is Harrison T. Filbert, Jr. All his good friends, however, called him Stinky (see fig. 16.12). Whenever his friends used the name, they were, of course referring only to Harrison—anything they said about or did to Stinky landed squarely on Harrison. Stinky became Harrison's alias, or assumed name.

Figure 16.12
Harrison T. Filbert, Jr. was better known by his alias, Stinky.

In the Macintosh, we can assign one or more aliases to any Desktop object (disk volume, folder, file, file server, and even the Trash). To create an alias, we first select the original item and choose Make Alias from the Finder's File menu (see fig. 16.13). An alias to an object appears at the same Desktop or folder level as a copy of the icon, with the item name displayed in italics. For added flexibility, we can change the name to anything we want—the alias file knows how to link back to its original at all times.

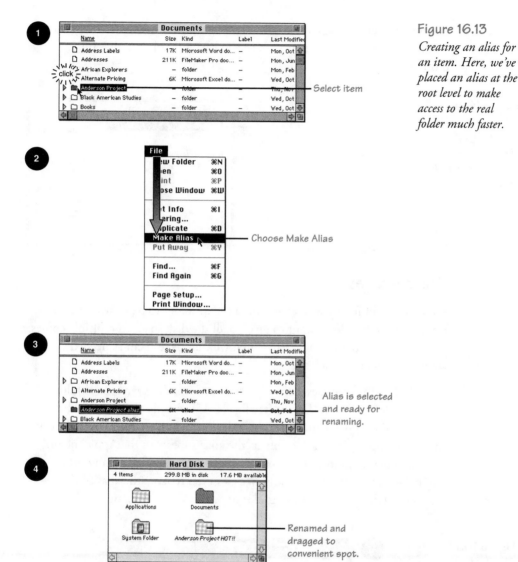

Figure 16.13
Creating an alias for an item. Here, we've placed an alias at the root level to make access to the real folder much faster.

The important attribute about an alias is that it does everything its original does (see fig. 16.14). Double-click an application's alias, and the application opens. Open a document alias from within an application, and the original document opens. Drag a file to the alias of a folder, and the file goes into the original folder. But drag an alias to the Trash, and only the alias file is trashed.

Figure 16.14
Aliases appear in File dialogs in italics. Treat them just like the items to which they belong.

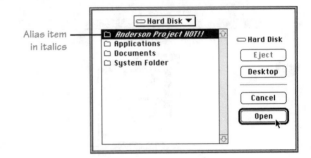

Using Aliases

Aliases come in handy when we want a file or folder to be in two or more places at once but don't want to give up all the disk space to multiple copies. Because aliases are tiny files (1 to 10K), we can make them as needed without sacrificing much space.

One ideal place for aliases is the *Apple Menu Items Folder*, a special folder found inside the System Folder (see fig. 16.15). Anything in that folder appears in the Apple menu (in alphabetical order). Therefore, if we place an alias to an application in that folder, the alias appears in the Apple menu. Choosing that item from the menu is the same as double-clicking the original—it starts the application. We can even rename the alias so that it means something more meaningful to us as we view the menu.

Figure 16.15
The Apple menu is a great place for aliases to frequently accessed items, such as applications.

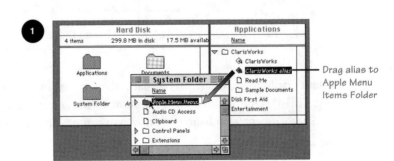

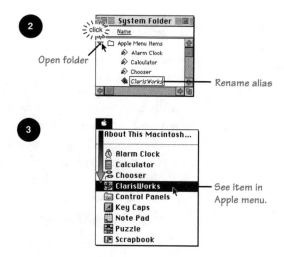

Automatically Starting Programs

We can use aliases in another special System Folder container called the *Startup Items Folder* (see fig. 16.16). Whenever the Mac starts up, it looks inside this folder for any icons to "double-click" (including aliases). Such items automatically start up when we start the Mac. For example, if one of your programs manages your daily calendar, it can start up with the Mac and be ready to show you today's appointments without any further effort on your part. This Startup Items Folder gizmo works with documents, as well. An alias to a specific database file in that folder both launches the program and loads the database during the startup process.

Startup Items

Figure 16.16
The Startup Items folder from the System Folder.

Different from DOS

The original IBM PCs weren't able to remember their clock settings when the power went off, but virtually every PC manufactured today has this feature. Setting the date and time, however, still requires typing some commands at the C:\> prompt. Changing other settings, which the Mac handles via control panels, often requires going through setup utilities or changing the CONFIG.SYS file. As for having programs start with the machine, you have to be comfortable with editing the AUTOEXEC.BAT file to make things happen.

They're Out To Get Us

Macintosh internal clocks remember their stuff with the help of a small battery inside the system unit. If this battery runs down, the clock won't hold its time and date. You'll likely see dates from the year 1904, the beginning of the Macintosh clock. Unfortunately, changing one of these batteries isn't like swapping a couple of AA cells in your Walkman. It may require taking the unit in for service. These batteries should last for many years, however.

It is still possible, with a good battery, for the clock to get jumbled up. Some other control panel settings (such as mouse tracking) may also go haywire. If this happens, hold down the magic four-key keyboard combination—Command-Option-P-R—during the Mac's startup to set everything back to zero (see fig. 16.17). You can reset those control panels again if you haven't contorted yourself into the chiropractor's office.

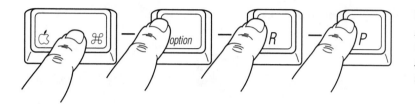

Figure 16.17
Pressing Command-Option-P-R during startup sets everything back to zero.

A common mistake when setting the clock is to forget to adjust the AM/PM setting. Thus, if it is really 10:30 AM but the clock gets set to 10:30 PM, the date will rollover at your real noon, because the Mac thinks it's midnight.

About the only alias gotcha is when you erase the original file or replace it with a file of a different name (like upgrading from *SuperScoop 2.0* to *SuperScoop 2.1*, and the version numbers are part of the file name). When this happens, a pleasant and helpful dialog alerts you to the fact that the original is missing (see fig. 16.18). It's time to trash the old alias and make a new one from the new original. No big deal.

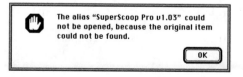

Figure 16.18
If the original file is missing or has been replaced by one with a different name, this alert tells us so.

Practice

Setting the Date

1. Choose Control Panels from the Apple menu. The Control Panels folder opens, revealing all those panels installed in your Mac.

2. Double-click on General Controls (see fig. 16.19).

Figure 16.19

Opening General Controls control panel.

General Controls

3. Click on the first (month) number in the date area.

4. Either click on the up or down arrows to cycle through the numbers or type the number of the current month.

5. Do the same for both the day and year numbers.

6. Click on the calendar icon to make these settings stick.

Setting the Time

1. Click on the hour number and type the current hour (unless it's only a couple minutes to the next hour, in which case type the next hour).

2. Click on the minutes number and type the digits for a couple of minutes in the future.

3. Click on the seconds number and type a zero.

4. Click on the AM or PM designation and type "A" or "P" depending on which side of noon the time will be set to.

5. If you are using a time standard (like the phone company's), call it up. Wait for the tone signaling the hour and minute in the setting and click the clock icon in synch (see fig. 16.20).

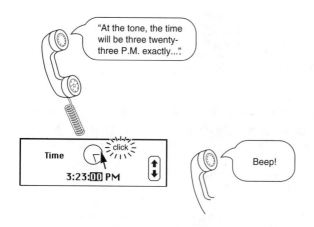

Figure 16.20
Setting the clock to a phone company time signal.

6. Close the General Controls window.

Setting Mouse Tracking

1. Open the Mouse control panel from the Control Panels folder (see fig. 16.21).

Figure 16.21
Opening the Mouse control panel.

2. Click on each Mouse Tracking setting and move the mouse around the desk to see how the pointer responds to your action. Select the setting that feels best for you.

3. Close the Mouse control panel.

Setting Volume and Beep Sound

1. Open the Sound control panel (see fig. 16.22).

Figure 16.22

Opening the Sound control panel.

2. Drag the slider control and release at several points along the track. Set the control to the desired setting. In a quiet office or at home, a lower volume may be all you need.

3. Click on each of the sounds in the listing at the right to sample each sound built into the Macintosh.

4. Choose the sound that you want to hear each time the Mac beeps at you.

5. Close the Sound control panel and the Control Panels window.

Summary

We have great control over the Macintosh's basic operations by adjusting control panels. If there is something about the way things look, feel, or sound that bothers you, the solution may be in a control panel. Aliases are small yet powerful stand-ins to other files, allowing us to place virtual copies of files anywhere we want for our own convenience.

Exorcises

1. How do you access control panels?

2. It's time to change all clocks to daylight saving time (turn clocks ahead one hour). Describe the steps required to keep the Macintosh clock in synch with local time.

3. What does it mean when the Macintosh beeps at you?

Sharing Information via Floppy Disk

Goal

Know how to transfer information from one Macintosh to another via SneakerNet.

What You Will Need

Macintosh turned on and at least one blank floppy diskette.

Terms of Enfearment

diskette	double-sided
diskette drive	high-density
floppy disk	eject
locked disk	SneakerNet
initialize	

Briefing

Mysterious Slit

If you haven't noticed already, almost every Mac has a horizontal slit on the front or side of the cabinet as shown in figure 17.1. (The exceptions are some PowerBook models.) This slit is the place for inserting a *diskette*—a hard, plastic-encased storage device (see fig. 17.2). Behind that slit is a *diskette drive*, the mechanism that writes and reads data to and from a diskette.

Figure 17.1
Most Macintosh models have a floppy disk drive.

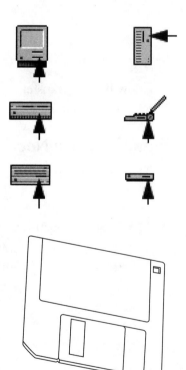

Figure 17.2
A Macintosh floppy disk.

A diskette stores information like a hard disk, but the diskette has much smaller capacity and is considerably slower in transferring data to and from it.

A diskette is also called a *floppy disk*, or just floppy. The actual disk material inside the plastic case is very pliable, but it's quite hazardous to the data on the disk when it bends. Dirt and oils from even our clean hands are equally dangerous—thus, the protective metal shutter that opens while the diskette is inside the computer.

Which Side Is Up?

Insert the metal shutter end first (see fig. 17.3). A debossed arrow on the top side of the diskette indicates how to insert the disk—with the arrow and label facing up. If the Mac is on its side, the diskette top usually faces to the left. It's not a big deal, because unless you try to force it, a diskette won't go in upside down or backwards.

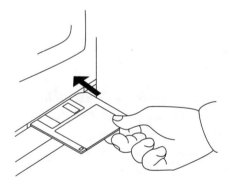

Figure 17.3
The proper way to insert a Macintosh floppy disk.

When you slip a disk into the drive slot, keep pushing it until you feel the drive grab it from you. The diskette should not be sticking out through the slot when it's properly seated.

A Plastic Lock

On the bottom side of the disk, opposite the beveled corner, is a locking tab (see fig. 17.4). The disk drive looks to this spot as you insert the disk to see whether the disk is *locked*—meaning that nothing new can be stored on the disk. If the tab is set so that you can see through the hole, the disk is locked.

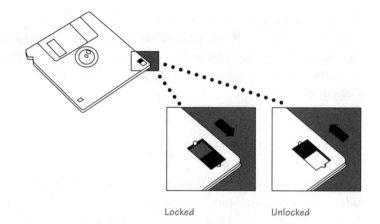

Figure 17.4
*You can lock a
floppy disk to protect
your data.*

Locked   Unlocked

To protect a diskette from accidental erasure or corruption, always lock the
disk before inserting it into the drive, unless you plan to copy information to
the disk.

A Really Blank Disk

For the Mac to locate and write information on a disk, the disk must be
mapped out just as a parking lot has lanes and spaces painted on it (see fig.
17.5). Truly blank disks are like a freshly paved, unpainted lot. The process
of setting up all those parking spaces for chunks of information is called
initializing (also known as *formatting* on other computers).

The Macintosh takes a proactive stance on uninitialized disks inserted into
the disk drive. If the disk is blank (or in a non-Macintosh format), a dialog
box asks whether we want to initialize the disk (see fig. 17.6). Choices
available to us depend on the storage capacity of the diskette we've inserted.

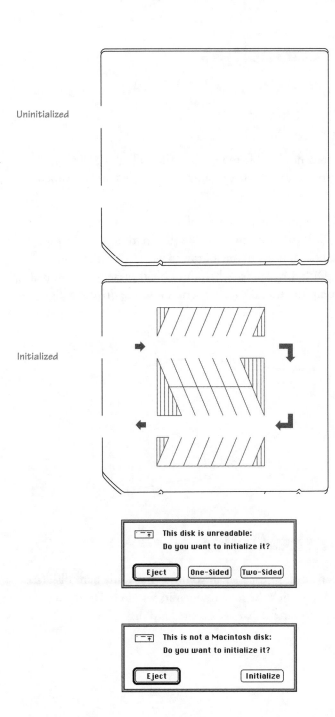

Uninitialized

Initialized

This disk is unreadable:
Do you want to initialize it?

[Eject] [One-Sided] [Two-Sided]

This is not a Macintosh disk:
Do you want to initialize it?

[Eject] [Initialize]

Figure 17.5
A blank disk is like an unpainted parking lot. Initialization lays out how and where information will be stored, just as parking lanes and spaces dictate where you can park your car.

Figure 17.6
A blank 800K disk may be initialized as single- or double-sided, but a 1.4M disk (bottom) can be formatted in one way only.

Two Disk Capacities

Floppy disks of the type the Mac accepts come in two styles and capacities:

Double-sided	800K
High Density	1.4M

Older Macintoshes may not be able to read or write to high-density diskettes, so the 800K style is the most common (and the disk size on which most software programs arrive).

High-density disks are immediately recognizable when we look at the diskette (see fig. 17.7). In addition to typical "HD" markings on the top side, an extra square hole appears in one of the corners (other than the locking tab corner). Disk drives sense when this hole is present and immediately signal to the computer that the disk inserted into the drive is a high-density one.

Figure 17.7
*High-density disks
are easily recognized.*

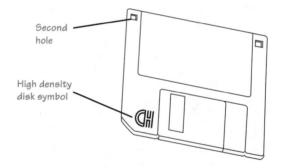

Second hole

High density disk symbol

What's on the Disk?

To the Finder, a floppy disk is just a small volume, like a tiny hard disk (see fig. 17.8). We can double-click the icon to open its window. On the disk may be icons of the same varieties we see on the hard disk.

Figure 17.8
Floppy disks are just small disk volumes, which may contain files, folders, and programs up to their capacity.

Ejecting the Disk

Perturbing though the idea may seem at first, the disk ejection process is handled by software, not by some button we push on the drive. Think of ejecting the diskette as removing it from the Desktop. Confusingly, the Macintosh makes us drag a floppy disk icon to the Trash to *eject* it (see fig. 17.9). This action does not harm or erase the diskette (a separate Special menu command, Erase Disk, is available for that) but triggers the drive to spit out the disk.

Figure 17.9
Dragging a disk icon to the Trash ejects the disk from the drive and removes the icon from the Desktop.

We may also eject diskettes from File Open and File Save dialogs when the floppy is the currently selected volume. The problem with this kind of ejection, however, is that it leaves a dimmed image of the diskette on the Desktop (see fig. 17.10). Nothing disastrous happens as a result, but numerous Desktop actions we make can cause the Mac to ask us to insert the diskette again. Feel free to insert and eject disks with a File dialog open; but when you next have a chance, switch to the Finder to drag all images of unneeded diskettes to the Trash.

Figure 17.10
Ejecting a disk from a file dialog lets us insert another to look for a file, but the icon of the ejected disk remains on the Desktop until we drag it to the Trash.

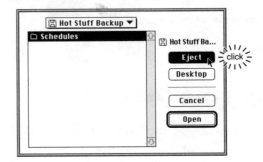

Copying a File to a Floppy

The point of this discussion was to show you how to copy a file to a floppy disk to share with another Mac user. After the disk is inserted (and initialized, if necessary), drag one or more files from the hard disk to the floppy disk icon (see fig. 17.11). A progress dialog lets us know how the copying is going (see fig. 17.12).

Figure 17.11
Drag selected file(s) to a floppy disk icon to copy the files. The originals are unharmed.

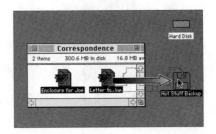

Figure 17.12
If the copy will take more than a couple of seconds, we see a progress dialog, which allows us to stop along the way.

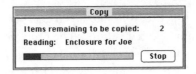

If we're trying to jam more stuff onto the diskette than it has room for, the Mac will alert us how many kilobytes we're over (see fig. 17.13). We'll have to copy fewer files to the disk and put the rest on another floppy.

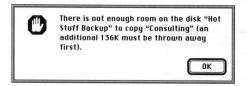

There is not enough room on the disk "Hot Stuff Backup" to copy "Consulting" (an additional 136K must be thrown away first).

OK

Figure 17.13
The Mac checks for sufficient space on the diskette before it begins the copy process. An alert box tells us how far off we are.

When we're done, we can put on our sneakers and speed our way to the colleague who needs the files—via *SneakerNet.*

Floppies as Backup

It's vital that we keep extra copies of documents some place other than the hard disk where they are normally stored. Then, if something dreadful should happen to the hard disk, we at least have a recent copy of important data.

Copying changed documents to floppy disks is one way to perform this backup operation. A number of commercial backup utility programs facilitate the process. Remember, however, that a full 80M hard disk could require as many as 57 high-density floppy disks for a complete backup—but far fewer just for your documents.

Floppy Copying

We've seen how to copy some files to a floppy. But, if we want to make an additional copy of that floppy disk, we use the Finder for that as well.

To start the process, we insert each diskette in turn to get diskette images of both on the Desktop at the same time. Here, we must use the Eject Disk

(Command-E) command in the Special menu, because dragging a diskette to the Trash removes its icon from the Desktop (see fig. 17.14).

Figure 17.14
For copying one floppy to another, we need the images of both on the Desktop. Use the Eject Disk menu command to eject a disk while leaving a shaded image on the Desktop.

Making sure that we know which is the source diskette, we drag that icon atop the destination icon (see fig. 17.15). A dialog box spells out in enormous detail what we're about to do and asks for confirmation (see fig. 17.16).

Figure 17.15
Drag the icon of the source disk to the icon of the destination disk.

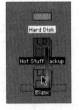

Figure 17.16
A dialog explains in great detail what is about to happen. Click OK to make it happen.

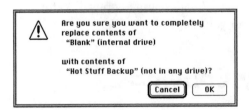

When the disk copying is completed, the destination disk contains the exact contents of the original, except that the disk name hasn't changed—we have to do that manually. The Finder allows multiple diskettes with the same name to appear on the Desktop, but it can get confusing quickly. Change the name and drag both icon images to the Trash to eject the disk in the drive and to remove both from the Desktop (see fig. 17.17).

Figure 17.17
Drag both icons to the Trash when copying is complete. Otherwise, things might get confusing.

Diskette Care

It's true that the hard, plastic shell around a floppy disk is durable, but the disk inside can be damaged by dirt, extreme heat or cold, crushing, strong magnetic fields, and moisture. If you're sharing a floppy via the mail, place the diskette in a padded diskette envelope for added safety. And don't use diskettes for dipping guacamole.

Different from DOS

A major departure from DOS is the way the Mac takes a proactive stand with an inserted disk. The machine knows immediately when you've inserted a disk and shows it on the Desktop. Only the machine can eject it (under your control). DOS disks, on the other hand, can be inserted or removed without the computer ever knowing anything about it. The computer won't know if the disk is unformatted or the wrong format until a program tries to read from or write to the disk. Disk formatting must also be handled by issuing the `format` command (and requisite command arguments depending on the disk capacity—something the Macintosh recognizes on its own).

continues

DOS and Macintosh systems lay down different parking lot arrangements when initializing their respective disks. With some software help (such as the Apple File Exchange software, which comes with the system software), a Macintosh can read from and write to a DOS diskette. This is only helpful if the programs on both the DOS and Macintosh computers can understand the same file format—something that is happening more and more.

They're Out To Get Us

The thorniest potential problem is a disk that gets trapped in the floppy disk drive when the power is off. To help keep things clear, the Mac automatically ejects the diskette upon shut down and upon start up (when the floppy doesn't contain any system software). But if the Mac should die completely, and you need the disk out of the floppy drive, it's time to unbend a low-tech paper clip. Insert one end into the tiny hole near the floppy drive slit (see fig. 17.18). Carefully and forcefully push the clip through the pinhole, to push a manual plunger that ejects the disk.

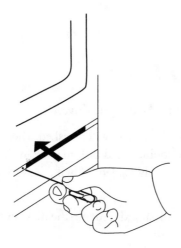

Figure 17.18
*Manually ejecting a
disk.*

Another quizzical event is when a diskette initialization fails (a dialog tells you so). If, after a second try, initialization still fails, it usually means that the disk has gone bad. Toss it in the real trash.

If you follow my advice and lock most floppy disks, you may try to save or copy a document to a diskette that is still locked (see fig. 17.19). An alert tells you all about it. Temporarily eject the disk, unlock the tab, and reinsert the disk. Now carry on.

Locked disk icon ────

Figure 17.19
*A padlock icon in a
Finder window
means that the
diskette is locked. We
may copy from a
locked disk, but
nothing can be
dragged to it.*

Finally, as on the hard disk, floppy disks don't give you all the space they have. Several kilobytes are occupied by hidden files that the system software uses to locate the parking spaces for each file.

Practice

Check Out a Disk

1. Insert a blank disk into the diskette drive.

2. If the disk is not initialized, you will be asked whether you want to initialize the disk. A double-sided disk may be initialized as single- or double-sided: choose double-sided. When asked to name the disk, type *Backup 1*.

3. If the disk is already initialized, rename the disk on the Desktop to *Backup 1* (see fig. 17.20).

Figure 17.20
Rename diskette to Backup 1.

4. Open the disk window (choose Icon from the View menu if it isn't in that view) and note the amount of space already occupied and how much is available.

5. Drag the diskette icon to the Trash. The disk ejects.

Copying to a Disk

1. Reinsert the *Backup 1* diskette.

2. Locate the Vacation Memo file on the hard disk and drag it to the *Backup 1* diskette.

3. Locate the Department Memos folder on the hard disk and drag it to the *Backup 1* diskette (see fig. 17.21).

4. Open the folder icon on the *Backup 1* diskette. The contents of the folder came along with the folder. Leave these windows open.

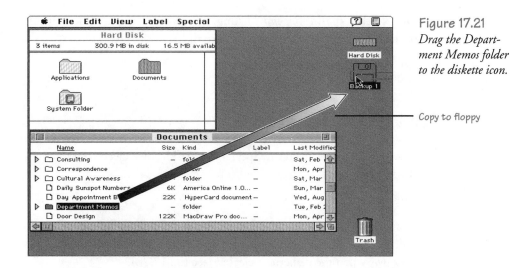

Figure 17.21
Drag the Department Memos folder to the diskette icon.

Copy to floppy

5. Locate the System Folder on the hard disk and drag it to the *Backup 1* diskette. Note the alert message that says there isn't enough space for everything. Click OK.

File Dialog Floppy

1. Launch TeachText and close the blank, untitled document window.

2. Choose Open from the File menu.

3. Click the Desktop button. The *Backup 1* diskette is listed as a volume on the Desktop.

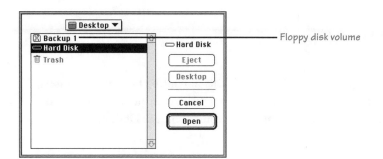

Floppy disk volume

Figure 17.22
The Backup 1 diskette appears as a volume on the Desktop in a file dialog listing.

4. Double-click on the *Backup 1* listing. The document and folder appear in the list, just as they would on a hard disk.

5. Click Cancel and quit TeachText.

How Not To Eject

1. Choose Eject Disk from the Special menu. The disk ejects, but a shaded icon remains on the Desktop.

2. Close all diskette windows.

3. Drag the diskette icon to the Trash. You are prompted to insert the disk, because the Macintosh wants to save the state of the active windows when the diskette is ejected (see fig. 17.23).

Figure 17.23
This dialog can appear frequently if we don't drag diskette icons to the Trash when we're finished with the diskettes.

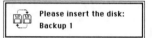

4. Insert the disk as requested. The Macintosh writes the window locations to the disk, ejects the disk, and removes its icon from the Desktop.

Summary

We've learned quit a lot about floppy disks, including how to lock, insert, and eject them. Copying files to or from a diskette is the same process as copying files to or from any Macintosh volume on the Desktop.

Exorcises

1. By what other names are 800K and 1.4M diskettes known?

2. What happens when you try to copy a 100K file to a floppy whose window is shown in figure 17.24?

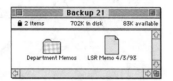

Figure 17.24
Drag a 100K file to this disk?

3. Is it possible to save a newly created document to a floppy disk instead of the hard disk?

4. If you drag a disk icon to the Trash to eject it, how do you erase an individual file from a diskette? How do you erase the diskette?

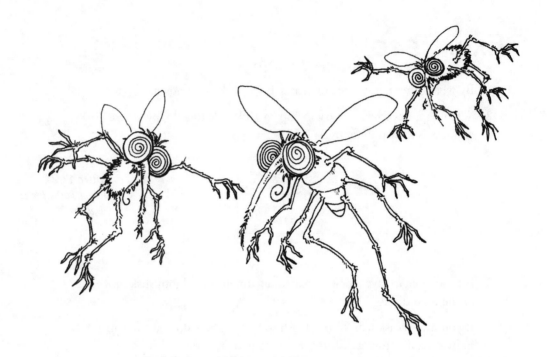

18th Encounter

Extending Your System's Capabilities

Goal

Gain familiarity with the Extensions, Control Panels, and Fonts folders inside the System Folder so that we can enhance our machines if we want to.

What You Will Need

Macintosh turned on.

Terms of Enfearment

extension	TrueType
INIT	PostScript
cdev	printer fonts
font suitcase	screen fonts

Briefing

A Never-Ending Story

As sophisticated as Macintosh system software is, we can actually think of its components as Lego blocks. Apple supplies a basic kit of parts that interlock nicely—so seamlessly that we scarcely notice the pieces. But to software developers, the Macintosh system is something that can be modified and enhanced with the addition of more components.

The bulk of these enhancements come in the form of *extensions*—software elements that automatically load into memory when the Macintosh starts up (see fig. 19.1). Extensions reside in the Extensions Folder inside the System Folder (see fig. 19.2). As each extension loads, it modifies or supplements the basic system software. For example, the Macintosh's capability to share files with others on a network is made possible by the combination of two Apple-supplied extensions: Network and File Sharing. Except for perhaps dropping these software elements into the System Folder, we never have to worry about them again. Their actions are automatic.

Figure 19.1

A generic extension icon indicates that an open series of items is possible.

Figure 19.2

The basic Extensions folder contains some Apple-supplied system extensions plus all printer drivers. Your folder may have additional items.

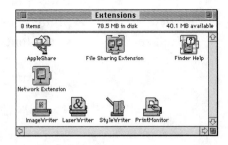

Extension Jargon

The term, *extension*, is relatively new in the Macintosh world. Previously this kind of file was known as an *INIT* (pronounced "in-IT"), and the term is still used quite a bit. Extension icons also sometimes appear along the bottom of the screen as each one loads during startup. Whether the icon appears is up to the extension's designer.

Extensions created by commercial or hobbyist developers perform a wide range of functions. Common ones include alarms, file compression utilities, menu enhancers, file dialog enhancers, and virus protectors (see fig. 19.3). All these functions must load before anything else happens on the Mac, because the processes they control tend to be running all the time behind the scenes.

Apple Photo Access

CD Remote INIT

Disinfectant INIT

Apple CD-ROM

CT Alarm

Figure 19.3
Examples of extension icons from Apple and other sources.

Control Panels, Too

Although we've seen how a few Apple-supplied control panels let us customize our environment, other control panels can also modify our Mac's behavior. For example, one popular control panel, called SuperClock, displays a digital clock in the menu bar. Upon opening the control panel, we have access to numerous preferences about how the clock should behave (see fig. 19.4). Like extensions, control panels load during start up if they need to (like SuperClock).

By the way, jargon for control panels is *cdev* (pronounced "SEE-dev"). The term comes from an internal naming convention of interest only to programmers and advanced users.

Figure 19.4
One dialog from the SuperClock! control panel gives us extensive flexibility over the digital time display in the menu bar.

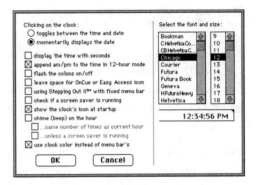

Typefaces and Fonts

One of the early hallmarks of the Macintosh was that it could reproduce on-screen (and on paper) a variety of typefaces akin to those used by professional typesetters. In Macintosh terminology, each typeface family is called a *font*. Virtually every text-oriented program allows us to select text and change the font, font size, and font style (e.g., plain, **bold**, *italic*). All fonts in the system are available to every program.

Macintosh fonts are nothing more than software elements—files in the System Folder. Actually, font files need to be in a special place for programs to recognize that they are there. Before System Version 7.1, fonts were part of the System File (in the System Folder). Beginning in late 1992 with Version 7.1, however, a special-purpose Fonts folder (still in the System Folder) is the holding place for font files (see fig. 19.5).

Figure 19.5
Most Macintosh font files belong in the Fonts folder, nested inside the System folder.

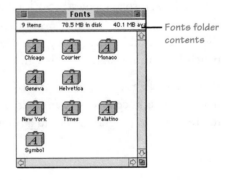

Fonts folder contents

Font Files Packed in a Suitcase

If we look in the Fonts folder, we see a number of icons that look like suitcases. Called, aptly enough, *font suitcase* files, they can contain one or more font specification files for that particular font (see fig. 19.6). Font suitcase files are convenient ways of copying entire font families from one machine to another. As for the precise content of a suitcase file, here's where things get sticky if precise font specifications are part of your work (e.g., for professional desktop publishing).

Suitcase file ———
contents

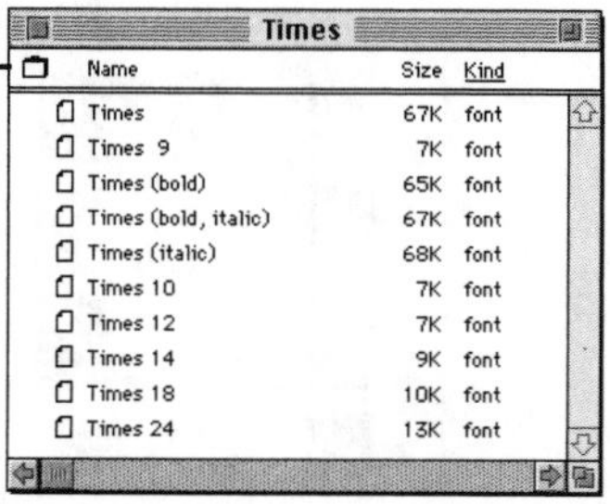

Times		
Name	Size	Kind
Times	67K	font
Times 9	7K	font
Times (bold)	65K	font
Times (bold, italic)	67K	font
Times (italic)	68K	font
Times 10	7K	font
Times 12	7K	font
Times 14	9K	font
Times 18	10K	font
Times 24	13K	font

Figure 19.6
A font suitcase file, such as Times, can contain several elements related to the font.

TrueType and PostScript

Confusing matters is that the Macintosh employs two font technologies. One is called *TrueType*; the other is called *PostScript* and was developed by a company called Adobe Systems. All the fonts supplied with the Macintosh system software are TrueType fonts and print fine results with all Apple branded printers, including the low-cost StyleWriter. Amid the individual files in a particular font's suitcase, such as the one shown in figure 19.7, are the font specifications that printouts require (*printer fonts*) plus several sizes of font for good-looking screen display (*screen fonts*).

You may have heard about PostScript if you have a LaserWriter, because networked LaserWriters all have PostScript built into them. For our discussion here, we can say that PostScript is another way a computer can render characters on the screen or in a printer (see fig. 19.8). Professional typesetting service bureaus prefer that their clients who produce the documents do so with PostScript fonts in their systems, because these fonts do the best job with the service bureaus' imagesetting machines.

Figure 19.7

A typical TrueType font suitcase contains font definitions (larger files) and screen fonts for most popular sizes.

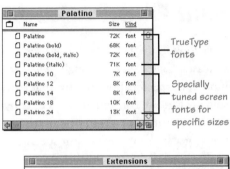

Figure 19.8

A sampling of PostScript printer font files, which must go in the Extensions folder. Screen font files for these fonts are also in the Fonts folder.

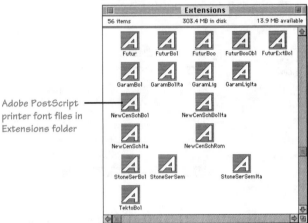

Adding Fonts

Additional fonts are available through Macintosh software dealers and mail order houses. Most collections are PostScript, but more TrueType font packages are reaching the shelves these days. For documents other than those requiring professional typesetting, any combination of TrueType and PostScript fonts works well on a PostScript-equipped LaserWriter; use TrueType exclusively for ImageWriter and StyleWriter output.

Smart System Folder

Even if we forget what goes where in the System Folder, the Macintosh helps us out. If we drag any item that belongs in a special folder to the System Folder icon (not to the open System Folder window), we receive a dialog message advising us that the item(s) belong in special folders (see fig. 19.9). The message asks us to confirm that we want the Mac to put these items where they belong. It's always best to let the Mac do this for us, because there is less chance for error. Anything that doesn't go into one of those special folders ends up inside the System Folder.

Extensions need to be stored in the Extensions folder in order to be available to the Macintosh. Put "Apple CD-ROM" into the Extensions folder?

[Cancel] [OK]

Figure 19.9
The System knows where items belong and alerts about where things are about to go.

Different from DOS

Extending a DOS machine's system capabilities is no simple task. If you're lucky, an installer of such a function will modify the AUTOEXEC.BAT or CONFIG.SYS files for you. Managing the whereabouts of any supplementary system files is up to you.

Fonts are an alien concept to DOS itself. If a program provides any font selection, the fonts are available only for that program. Moreover, the fonts can't be exchanged with other programs. Windows, however, provides system-wide font management somewhat along the lines of the Mac.

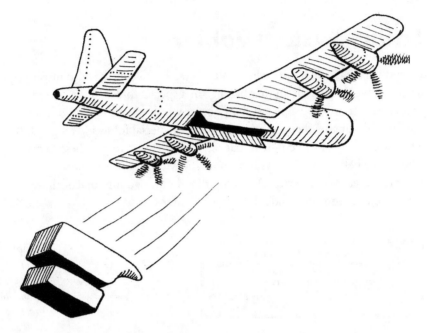

They're Out To Get Us

Probably, the biggest source of head scratching by Macintosh users is when an extension conflict plagues the system. Symptoms usually include a system hang or system error dialog (signified by the bomb icon in the dialog).

Extensions can conflict with each other or with an application (or even just a single process in an application). Tracking down these conflicts can be a tedious process if your Macintosh has many extensions installed. See the 20th Encounter for tips on how to do this.

Practice

Exploring the System Folder

1. Open the System Folder. Notice the other folders within (see fig. 19.10). Those with special icons are the system's special-purpose folders.

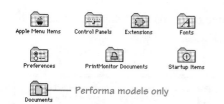

Figure 19.10
*Special-purpose
folders inside the
System folder.*

2. Locate each of the following files in their associated folder and drag the
files to the Desktop:

Folder	File
Control Panels	Map control panel
Apple Menu Items	Key Caps desk accessory
Fonts	Monaco font suitcase
Extensions	File Sharing Extension

3. Close all windows except the hard disk window and bring the System
Folder icon into view.

4. Select all four files you just dragged to the Desktop.

5. Drop them onto the System Folder. Read the message that asks
whether they should go where they belong (see fig. 19.11).

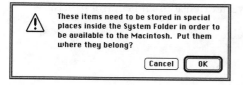

Figure 19.11
*Drop items onto the
System Folder and
let the System figure
out where everything
goes.*

6. Click OK. Read the second message that tells you what the Macintosh did with the four files (see fig. 19.12). Click OK.

Figure 19.12
Afterward, you get a report of what went where.

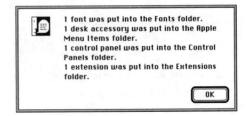

1 font was put into the Fonts folder.
1 desk accessory was put into the Apple Menu Items folder.
1 control panel was put into the Control Panels folder.
1 extension was put into the Extensions folder.

OK

Summary

We've seen that the Macintosh consists of a set of software pieces that we decide we need. By adding items to special folders—especially Extensions and Control Panels—we can add functions to the basic Macintosh operation we use every day. That includes extending the selection of fonts for our text-based documents.

Exorcises

1. Describe the differences between extensions and control panels.

2. What happens when you double-click each of the following system items?

extension
control panel
font suitcase
font file
desk accessory

3. We've seen why a font suitcase file is called a suitcase and has an icon to match. Why does the System file also have a suitcase icon as shown in figure 19.13?

System

Figure 19.13
System file suitcase.

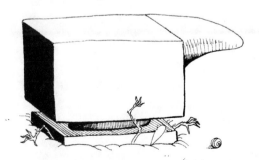

19th Encounter

When Things Don't Work

Goal

Learn how to track down sources of problems so that you can solve them yourself or ask the right questions.

What You Will Need

Lots of luck to never need information in this encounter.

Terms of Enfearment

bomb
bug
crash
hang
freeze
#&*%@!

Briefing

On the Edge

Using a personal computer in our work can truly improve the quality and quantity of work we accomplish. But, try as we might to regard the computer as just another tool, the technology can really grab us by the neck when things don't work. Moreover, we must contend with Danny Goodman's corollary to Murphy's Law:

> If something goes blooey on the computer, it happens when we have the least amount of time to deal with the problem.

The closer a deadline nears, the more likely a computer foul-up will gum up the works.

When Most Problems Occur

It's rare for a computer to go haywire by just sitting there on its own. If something breaks, it generally happens when we try to start the computer or when we issue a command for the computer or software program to do something. Because problems manifest themselves in response to our actions, it is not uncommon for us to blame ourselves, rather than the computer.

Admitting There Is a Problem

The good news is that every problem has a solution. Some solutions are easier than others, but the problems can be solved.

When something unexpected occurs, we'll arrive at a solution if we do our best to narrow down the possible sources of the difficulty. Nine out of ten problems can be solved or worked around on our own. Even if the problem ultimately results in having to take the computer into the shop, the better we can define the problem, the quicker (and cheaper) the repair will likely be.

Get Terminology Right

If we plan to tell anybody about the problem, it is vital to describe the general symptom properly. Too many times effort goes into tracking a symptom when the user misnamed the problem. Use the following handy table:

What Happens	What To Call It
All action stops, except rolling mouse pointer	hang or freeze
Everything freezes, including pointer	system crash
Screen goes psychedelic	system crash
System error dialog box (see fig. 20.1)	bomb
Hard disk won't mount for love or money	disk crash
Something you didn't expect	bug
`Error in script` dialog (see fig. 20.2)	HyperCard script error
Any of the preceding resulting in lost data	#&*%@!

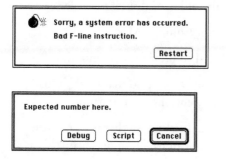

Figure 20.1
*System error—
a real bomb.*

Figure 20.2
*HyperTalk script
error dialog.*

Find What Works

When a problem prevents us from continuing with our work, we must begin looking for a diagnosis—at last, a chance to be the doctor our parents always wanted us to be. Assuming that the computer worked properly at some time before the problem occurred, the first task is to try to get back to the state in which things worked.

The simple fact is that a lot of problems occur when we add something new to our computer—a new hard disk, new software, a new extension. Although the new thing may not be the real cause of the problem (the problem may be lurking, ready to leap out because of a conflict with the new item), we must reach a point at which we can safely say that adding so-and-so causes the problem.

> **Word of Warning:** Before you start connecting and disconnecting cables or opening the lid of your Mac, turn off the machine (and unplug it from the power outlet if you're sticking your fingers inside the case). I want you to be alive to finish reading this book.

If we've added any of the following new items, we should perform the corresponding action as a first step in diagnosis:

New Item	Action
External hard disk	Disconnect it from the Mac
Internal hard disk	Reinstall the old hard disk, if possible
Any external device	Disconnect it from the Mac
RAM module	Restore RAM to previous configuration
Extension	Drag it to the Desktop so that it won't load with other extensions upon startup
Control Panel	Drag it to the Desktop so that it won't load with other control panels upon startup

New Item	Action
Font	Drag it to the Desktop so that it won't load with other fonts upon startup
Application or DA	Don't launch it

This advice can be tricky at times, because an application may come with an extension or control panel that has been unknowingly installed into the System Folder stuff. There may also be another Murphy's Law corollary in the wings, because it's eerily common for us to buy more than one new thing at a time and to install or connect them all in a rush. The key here, however, is to get all the new stuff out of the line of fire and to make sure that we've returned to a reliable state. Then gradually add back each item one at a time and try to recreate the problem. When the problem recurs, the last item just added is the most likely suspect.

Probably Problems

We'll now examine the five most common symptoms of trouble and describe how best to isolate the cause for each. Unless you're faced with one of these problems, it's not important to read each in full detail. It may be helpful, however, to read through the symptoms: if one should happen to your Mac, you'll know where to turn for help.

Really, Really Dead

Symptom

When you press the on switch for the Mac, absolutely nothing happens: no tones, no screen illumination, no disk spinning.

Nature of the Problem

Either the Mac is completely fried, or the Mac isn't getting power.

First Thoughts

After the initial anxiety that the Mac may be roadkill, it's more likely a case of a loose keyboard cable or power cord.

What To Do

1. Make sure that you are attempting to turn on the Mac the proper way for your model. Your Mac model may start via a rear panel switch or button.

2. For PowerBooks, plug in the AC adapter. The battery may be fully discharged.

3. For Macs that start from the keyboard "on" switch, make sure that the keyboard is securely cabled to the Mac's desktop bus connector on the rear panel.

4. Make sure that the Mac is plugged into a live power outlet (test the outlet with another electrical item if necessary).

5. Try substituting other keyboard and power cables, because a break in a cable could prevent it from carrying the requisite juice or *on* signal.

6. Contact your dealer about service (always the last resort).

Alive, but Barely

Symptom

The Mac turns on, but instead of hearing the usual startup tone or chord, you either hear a sequence of tones at full volume or see a Macintosh icon with a sad face in it (see fig. 20.3).

Figure 20.3
Sad Mac icon.

Nature of the Problem

Your Mac failed the hardware self-test it performs each time you turn on the machine. Either a component on the system board inside the computer has gone bad (very unlikely) or something isn't connected correctly.

First Thoughts

This problem occurs predominantly after you've added something new in the hardware department: RAM modules inside the system or any device connected to the SCSI ("scuzzy") port (see fig. 20.4). In the case of RAM modules (called SIMMs), they are either installed in the wrong order (each Mac has its own peculiar way of accommodating SIMMs), are the wrong type of SIMM for your Mac model, or they aren't seated properly in their sockets. For SCSI devices, the problem could be many things (see "SCUZZY WUZZY"), but tightening a loose cable takes care of 90 percent of the problems. Be sure, however, to begin the diagnosis by removing all new items and making sure that the original setup works properly.

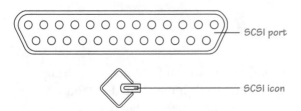

SCSI port

SCSI icon

Figure 20.4
Check the cable connected to the SCSI port.

What To Do

1. If you've just added some new hardware or moved things around, restore the old scene to see whether the old way works. Gradually add new items back to the system until you encounter the problem.

2. Make sure that all SCSI cables (if any) are securely fastened to their connectors.

3. Make sure that all memory SIMM modules are squarely seated in their sockets.

4. Make sure that all system board connectors are squarely seated in their sockets.

Disk, Please!

Symptom

The Macintosh turns on, but instead of your hard disk spinning and the Desktop appearing on the screen, all you see is the Mac icon with the flashing question mark in it (see fig. 20.5).

Figure 20.5
Flashing question mark means that the Mac can't find any disk with a System file on it.

Nature of the Problem

Your Mac can't locate a disk that has system software on it.

First Thoughts

It's either something very simple (like an external SCSI device not being turned on) or a potentially serious problem with the hard disk. You will want to have backed up everything the night before—but of course, you didn't.

What To Do

1. Make sure that all SCSI devices are turned on and have power before turning on the Mac.

2. Insert a floppy disk that has a minimum system on it. If this fails, manually switch off the Macintosh and try starting again with the floppy disk. Try this once again but disconnect any cable attached to the SCSI port. If this last attempt doesn't make it, it's time for service, and you can skip the rest of this section.

3. If your Mac doesn't have an internal hard disk, connect only the desired startup hard disk to the Macintosh. Turn on the hard disk and wait about 30 seconds before turning on the Mac.

4. Check the external hard disk's SCSI ID number (usually controlled by a numbered switch on the rear of the hard disk). It should be a number between one and six (inclusive) and be different from any other SCSI device connected to the computer.

5. For an external disk drive, try another SCSI cable, if one is available; for an internal drive, make sure that all cables between the drive and system board are securely fastened to their connectors.

6. After starting the Mac with a floppy disk, use whatever backup method you prefer to make copies of irreplaceable files. The next steps may make it more difficult to recover files if the disk is damaged.

7. Run the *Disk First Aid* program, which comes with the system software. This program tries to fix simple problems with hidden files on the disk that the computer needs. If the program reports that it has fixed one or more problems, try restarting the Mac; if the program reports that there are problems it can't fix, proceed to step 9.

8. Restart the Mac, while pressing and holding the Command, Option, P, and R keys simultaneously. This action clears some internal settings, including one that dictates where the Mac should look for a system disk (the information may have become so corrupted that only zapping it with this key sequence will help it recover).

9. Obtain a disk recovery program, such as Norton Utilities for the Macintosh (Symantec Corp.) or Disk Tools (Central Point Software). Follow instructions for the product to perform a disk diagnosis. The products will also attempt to repair the damaged files

10. If the disk drive you're trying to start from is not supplied by Apple as part of the computer, a diskette of hard disk formatting software should have accompanied the drive. If you don't have this software, obtain a copy of a hard disk utility program, such as Hard Disk ToolKit Personal Edition (FWB Software, Inc.). Follow the directions to let the software make sure that the disk driver (a piece of hidden software that smoothes communication between your hard disk and the Mac) is up to date. This software should be able to identify your hard disk's manufacturer and model number to make sure that the proper driver is installed.

11. If possible, try the disk drive (even if it's an internal drive) on another Macintosh. There is the remote possibility (hey, this is the time to grasp at straws) that the system board is faulty, preventing *any* hard disk from booting.

12. With your backup files carefully saved from the hard disk, use the disk formatting software supplied with your hard disk (Disk First Aid for Apple-supplied drives or the formatting utility that comes with after-market drives). If the formatting fails, proceed to the next step; otherwise reinstall the System software and restore your files from the backup.

13. If you've reached this far and can't get that disk working, you're in big trouble, we're sorry to say. The disk is so badly damaged that you'll need to send the disk to a disk recovery service. The disk drive's manufacturer may provide such a service or direct you to a company that performs the service. Most or all of your data files are probably still intact on the disk, and some disk recovery services charge according to the number of files you ask them to save (but you have to be able to tell them which files they are).

Welcome to Ma...

Symptom

The Macintosh turns on, the hard disk spins, and the Welcome To Macintosh dialog appears. Some extension icons may start appearing across the bottom of the screen, and then everything stops dead.

Nature of the Problem

One or more extension and control panels are conflicting with each other or with the system software.

First Thoughts

You want to make sure that the Mac, itself, is OK, so you try turning on the Mac with all extensions off.

What To Do

1. Power down the machine manually. Hold down the Shift key and start the Macintosh (see fig. 20.6). This turns on the Mac but bypasses the process that loads extensions and control panels. You get a virgin system running. If the machine still freezes, work through the next section, "HangUps."

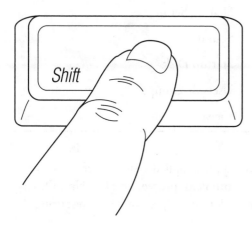

Figure 20.6
Holding down Shift while starting the Macintosh bypasses the process that loads extension and control panels.

2. Drag all non-Apple-supplied extensions and control panels from their
   folders to the Desktop (or to a new folder you create on the Desktop to
   help keep them together). The following table is a list of safe Apple-
   supplied items you can leave in their folders:

System Extensions	Control Panels
AppleShare	Backlight Control
Caps Lock	Color
File Sharing Extension	Date & Time
Network Extension	File Sharing Monitor
	General Controls
	Keyboard
	Labels
	Map
	Memory
	Monitors
	Mouse
	Network
	Numbers
	PowerBook
	Sharing Setup
	Sound
	Startup Disk
	Users & Groups
	Views

Restart the Mac with only the Apple-supplied system extensions and
control panels. If there is still a problem, proceed to HangUps. Otherwise, begin adding each item back to its respective folder, restarting the

Mac each time. When the Mac freezes during the startup process, the last item you added is the culprit.

3. Write down all extensions and control panels in those folders and contact the manufacturer of the culprit. Select the file in the Finder and choose Get Info from the File menu to view a copyright notice (see fig. 20.7). A more recent version of the offending file may clear up the problem.

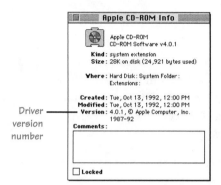

Driver version number

Figure 20.7
External device driver files usually contain version numbers in their Get Info dialog boxes.

4. If the problem extension is related to an external device (e.g., CD-ROM player, scanner), contact the manufacturer of the device. Be prepared to tell them which version of the driver you have (from the Get Info dialog).

Hangs and Bombs (Not a Law Firm)

Symptom

While performing an action in the Finder or application, the Macintosh freezes or presents the system error dialog box (the latter often displaying some incomprehensible message, such as bad F-line instruction).

Nature of the Problem

Although we don't doubt there's a problem, if the problem isn't repeatable, it will be virtually impossible to diagnose or get help. It could be a program bug (unlikely), a conflict between the program and an extension, or a problem between the program and some external device. A commercial problem solver utility program, such as Help! (Teknosys), may be able to track the cause for you.

First Thoughts

The worst part about this kind of problem is that everything you've done to a document since it was last saved is lost to the cosmos (#&*%@!), so you probably begin from a deficit position. One of the best ways to quickly diagnose and track this kind of problem is to recall the precise steps you went through before the freeze or bomb.

What To Do

1. If the keyboard or mouse is ineffective, suspect the keyboard cable. For a quick remedy, try unplugging the mouse and keyboard cables (without turning off the Mac in this extreme case) and then reconnecting them. If you now have regained control, consider replacing the keyboard cable. If this doesn't work, try another keyboard cable, if you have one available.

2. For a program freeze, try pressing Command-Period in case the program is caught in some kind of loop that has a user-controllable exit built into it. If the pointer returns to normal and if you can pull down menus, you're back in business.

3. If that doesn't work, try pressing Command-Option-Escape to force the current application to quit (see fig. 20.8). Click the Force Quit button in the dialog box. If this works, you'll regain control of the

Mac, but it's possible that RAM contents have been boggled a bit. Immediately save documents in other applications, quit those applications, and restart the Mac.

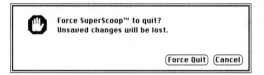

Figure 20.8
Command-Option-Escape leads to the Force Quit dialog to exit a frozen program.

4. If a Force Quit just completely hangs the system, it's System Crash City. Manually restart the Mac via the Reset button (if your Mac model has one accessible). Occasional rare and spectacular crashes won't even let the Reset button work, in which case you've got to hit the big switch (or button) on the back of your Mac that forces the machine to shut down. You can then start the machine as usual.

5. For a true bomb, the dialog box offers a Restart button. Click it. Quite often, you'll just crash and have to go through step 3.

6. Turn off the Macintosh and check all cables connected to the Mac, especially AppleTalk and SCSI cables. Make sure that they're all connected securely all the way down the chain of devices.

7. If the problem persists, try starting the Macintosh with all extensions off (holding down the Shift key). Try to recreate the problem if you can. The problem is probably a bug in the program. Call the software publisher about the problem. When a problem is repeatable only when extensions are turned on, then it will be necessary to go through the extension-sifting process described in "Welcome To Ma...," to find the conflict (or let a program such as Help! assist in the process). The problem could be in either the extension or the program. Typically, the more recently published product is responsible for working with other

things out on the market, but it isn't always possible for a developer to test every combination of extension and control panel for compatibility. Contact the program's publisher with the name of the conflicting extension, and see whether the company can figure out a solution. In the meantime, you'll have to decide which is more valuable: the function added by the extension or the productivity gained by the application. Use the one that you need most.

Scuzzy Wuzzy

Macintosh problems caused by SCSI-related difficulties are sometimes incredibly difficult to resolve. As you add SCSI devices to the chain, the steps required to find a solution can grow exponentially.

If you suspect a SCSI-related problem, here are the first things to check before getting too technical:

1. Turn off the Mac and all devices and make sure that all cables are securely locked onto their connectors. If the connector has clips, clip them; if the connector has screws, tighten them.

2. Before turning on the Macintosh, turn on all SCSI devices and give them about 30 seconds to get up to speed.

3. If the device requires any software (drivers), be sure that the version of the driver file you have is compatible with the version of the system software you're running. If not, get the latest driver from the device manufacturer.

4. Check the number switches on the rear panel of all SCSI devices and make sure that each one is set to a different number (in any order) and that none of them is set to zero (reserved for an internal SCSI hard disk) or seven (the Mac system board's ID). Try a different numbering order if one set doesn't work.

5. Finally, try connecting the devices in a different order, provided your cable runs allow it. If the SCSI cables you have are of different lengths (and especially if one of them is something like 10 feet long), try different length cables in different positions along the chain.

When a problem persists after you've gone through these steps, it's time to get creative with the SCSI cables and the double-edged connector called a SCSI terminator (see fig. 20.9). A terminator attaches to a SCSI connector on a SCSI device and can, when necessary, be placed between the cable and the device (i.e., both the cable and terminator lead to only one of the two SCSI connectors on the device).

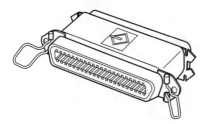

Figure 20.9
A SCSI terminator can be placed between a cable and a SCSI device.

The last device on a SCSI chain must usually have a terminator on the unused SCSI connector (i.e., it "terminates" the SCSI cabling chain). Occasionally, a device may have a terminator built into it, but that fact won't be readily apparent by looking at the device. In either case, try the following steps (turning off all devices while changing cables each time and restarting the Mac to see whether things work OK):

1. Remove the terminator from the last device.

2. Reintroduce the terminator to the SCSI chain, starting at the location between the SCSI cable and the connector of the last device.

3. For each attempt, move the terminator one step closer toward the Mac: first to the outgoing connector of the next-to-last device; then to the incoming connector; and so on (see fig. 20.10).

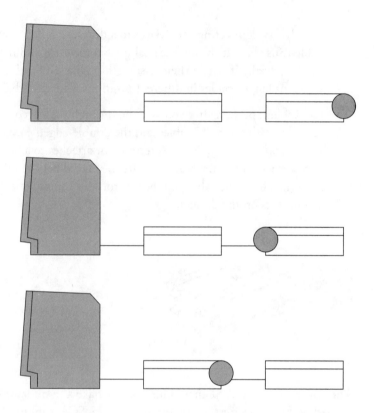

Figure 20.10
Testing the terminator at various locations.

Some users have gone through all this and still were unable to keep all devices in the chain working. In these extreme cases, it may be necessary to remove one or more items from the chain and to connect them only when needed. It's not a great solution, but a solution nevertheless.

20th Encounter

Avoiding Computing Disasters: Rules To Live By

Goal

Establish automatic behavior patterns that prevent catastrophes.

What You Will Need

One ounce of prevention.

Terms of Enfearment

virus
surge protector

Briefing

If you glanced through the last encounter, your anxiety level may be up a notch or two. Some of those problems seem like genuine nightmares. Although no one or no magical device can guarantee that you won't experience some of the problems described there, you can pattern your work habits with the Macintosh to minimize the risk of those things happening.

Yes, it's something of an added burden to have to think about these extra tasks, but it's a price everyone pays for using technology. With that, I present a succinct list of little things you can do to prevent lost work or time.

1—Backup Your Data Regularly

A daily backup of your documents is the best insurance against a loss. No matter what else may befall your Macintosh, the backup copies will allow you to restore your machine to the state of its last backup. A number of commercial backup utility programs ease the burden. With a tape drive or extra hard disk that is at least as capacious as the main one you use, the backup program could do the job while you're out to lunch or while you're getting ready to leave for the day.

> **Performa owners note:** Because your Mac does not come with a set of system diskettes, it's vital that you use the Apple Backup program (in the Launcher window) to create a copy of your System Folder (one of the options). You can then use the Apple Restore program (from the Utilities disk) to reinstall the system software in case one of its files should become corrupted by a virus or malfunction.

2—Invest in Virus Detection Software

A *virus* is the generic term for evil little software gremlins designed by clever and sadistic computer programmers. Viruses propagate silently from machine to machine primarily through the sharing of files via floppy disks (the source machine must be infected) or the transfer of files from databases over the telephone (the files are infected, and the virus spreads when the file is opened on your machine).

Viruses are sometimes benign—playing some trick on the user, such as displaying a funny message when it shouldn't. More often, viruses are dangerous, corrupting important system files, documents, programs, and even erasing a hard disk without warning.

Virus detection software usually includes a system extension that always runs as you use the Mac. If it detects any of the hidden actions that viruses tend to perform, it alerts you to potential danger and can prevent the damage. Such software can also scan your hard disk(s) to see whether any known viruses are already on your disk and remove them if so.

3—Keep an Emergency System Floppy Disk Handy

The bulk of hard disk problems prevent the disks from starting the Macintosh. All the applications and documents on the disk tend to be in fine shape, but at first glance, you may think you can't get to them. If you can start the Mac from a floppy disk, the hard disk will more than likely appear as a second volume on the Desktop, beneath the floppy startup disk icon. But, the only way that will happen is if you have an emergency floppy disk handy. The system software installer (not included with Performas) includes a Customize option for creating a minimum system diskette—just the ticket (see fig. 21.1). For Performa users, a copy of the Utilities disk acts as an emergency disk.

Figure 21.1
Use the Customize section of the system software installer to create a minimum system diskette.

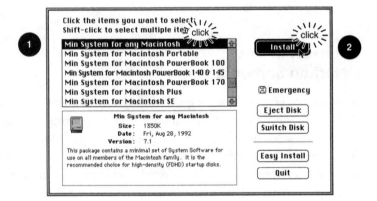

4—Invest in a File Recovery Utility Program

There will be a time—guaranteed—when you will have erased a file that you desperately need again. Nothing that comes with the Macintosh system software will get that file back for you. But, if you haven't done a lot of disk writing since you trashed the file (or there is plenty of space on your disk), a commercial file recovery program has an excellent chance of un-erasing the file for you.

File recovery software, in the form of products such as Norton Utilities for the Macintosh (Symantec Corp.) and Disk Tools (Central Point Software) provide a number of helpful utility programs for recovering damaged hard disks. These products tend to pay for themselves the first time they save your butt.

5—Rebuild Your Desktop Periodically

The Desktop relies on two hidden hard disk files to help the Finder keep track of documents and their applications. In normal operation, these files get bigger the more you add and delete files. A good practice is to instruct the Mac to rebuild this file from scratch every few weeks. To do this, hold down the Command and Option keys while the Mac starts up. Eventually, a dialog box lets you confirm the request to rebuild (see fig. 21.2). Rebuilding can take several minutes on a large hard disk.

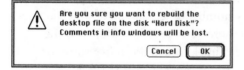

Figure 21.2
This alert asks us to confirm that we want to rebuild the Desktop file. Few files, if any, have comments that will be lost.

6—Lock Read-Only Floppy Disks

One reason we recommended earlier that you lock floppy disks that won't be written on is to prevent virus infection (see fig. 17.4). For example, you wouldn't want a virus to infect a master disk of an application program (which could happen as easily as inserting the diskette and opening the disk window), in case you need to re-install that program.

Occasionally, a program won't let you install itself from a locked floppy disk. In that case, lock the original and make a duplicate of the original. Install the software from an unlocked copy.

7—Turn Everything Off before Plugging or Unplugging Cables

Some users go forever swapping SCSI cables without powering down without a problem. This is risky business, especially for SCSI cables. Worse yet, when cable switching with the power on causes a problem, it is often a case of a blown component on the Mac's system board—an expensive repair proposition.

8—Invest in a Surge Protector

Surges are the generic term for a number of different types of zaps from the power company. They occur for any number of reasons, all of which are out of your control: switching electrical sources in the power grid; restoring power after a blackout; a power pole being knocked down in a storm or accident; heavy electrical equipment on the same line being cycled on or off. A surge protector tries to intercept the very brief, very high voltage zaps before they reach devices plugged into them.

9—Unplug Everything in an Electrical Storm if Power Lines Are above Ground

A direct lightning strike to a power pole feeding your place of computing will fry most surge protectors and everything plugged into them. But, even a nearby hit can conduct enough juice in power lines to cause problems. The power lines act like a receiving antenna for energy given off by a lighting bolt, passing the jolt right to your power outlets. Even though equipment is turned off, at least one of the lines of the AC power cord remains connected to the circuitry of your Mac, providing a nice pathway for a shocker.

10—Keep at Least One Megabyte Available on Your Hard Disk

It's easy to forget to look at the amount of free disk space, because for many months your disk has more than ample room. But, when it starts to fill up, leave some breathing room for yourself. For one thing, you want to make sure that there's room for a new document you create and want to save. Secondly, some programs or processes, such as background printing and FAX software, write temporary files to the hard disk while they work with your documents: without the free space, the programs may not be able to complete some operations.

11—Load Your Constant Applications First

If you tend to keep one or more programs running all day, load them first thing upon startup (or put aliases of them in the Startup Items Folder). By occupying their memory blocks early, they will leave maximum contiguous memory available for other programs that may come and go during the day.

12—Avoid Temperature Extremes for PowerBooks

With a PowerBook tucked in a briefcase, you may forget that it's been left in a hot car or lugged across a frozen city. Although the machines are built to withstand extremes when not in use, the acceptable temperature range for using things like the hard disk and liquid crystal display is much narrower. If you bring a PowerBook indoors after it has been sitting for awhile in extreme heat or cold, open the lid and let the machine adjust to near room temperature before starting it up.

These aren't exactly 12 commandments, but they're certainly a dozen good guidelines to avoid Macintosh headaches. The sooner you take care of items 2 through 4 and build items 1, 5, 6, 7, and 11 into your computer routines, the sooner you can forget about the computer and comfortably get on with your work.

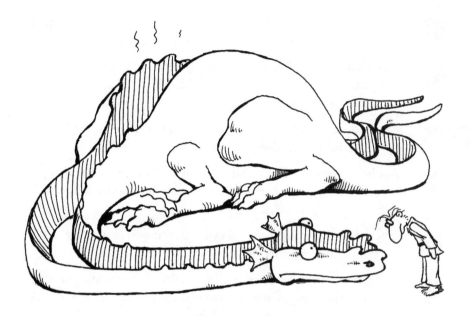

Glossary

The terms defined in this glossary were introduced in encounters throughout the book. The icons next to each term identify the encounter in which you will find the term used in context.

7   **active window** The topmost Finder or document window denoted by horizontal stripes in its title bar.

16   **alias** A small file that stands in for any volume, folder, or file located elsewhere on the hard disk or network.

5   **Apple menu** The leftmost menu bar item, enabling quick access to desk accessories and other programs, documents, or file servers (or their aliases) located in the Apple Menu Items folder.

16   **Apple Menu Items folder** A special purpose folder nested inside the System Folder. Items here appear in the Apple menu.

15   **AppleTalk** The built-in networking system that enables Macintoshes to communicate with each other and with networked printers.

8 **10**   **application** Usually a full-fledged software program (as distinguished from a *desk accessory*).

5   **Application menu** The menu at the right of the menu bar that enables quick switching between multiple applications running at the same time.

8   **autoscrolling** Scrolling a window by dragging an item in the direction you want the window to scroll.

15   **background printing** A process that enables the computer to send individual pages of a document to the printer while you work on other programs or documents.

12   **backup** An extra copy of a file to be used in case the original file becomes lost or damaged.

16   **beep sound** The sound the Macintosh makes when the machine or a program wants the user's attention.

14   **bitmap** A collection of pixels that form a graphic image.

19   **bomb** A system-level problem that causes all unsaved work to be lost.

2 **10**   **booting** Starting up a computer or program.

19   **bug** A problem, usually in application software, that causes the computer to do something other than what the program was designed to do.

12   **button** On the mouse, the area you press to execute a mouse click; on the screen, an area that is to be metaphorically pressed by positioning the screen pointer atop that area and pressing the mouse button.

18 cdev A control panel file.

15 Chooser A desk accessory that enables you to select a printer driver, connect to a networked printer, or activate networking services.

4 click A quick press and release of the mouse button.

14 Clipboard A special area of memory that temporarily holds any information copied or cut.

13 close The action of removing a window from the screen.

7 close box The clickable box in the upper left corner of most windows that enables you to close that window.

1 Command key A special-purpose keyboard key used in concert with one or more other character keys to issue commands to programs.

5 command-key equivalent The keyboard sequence (including the Command key) that performs the same action from the keyboard as choosing a menu item.

1 Control key A special-purpose keyboard key used in concert with one or more other character keys, used primarily for telecommunications programs.

16 control panel A software element that enables users to adjust system-level settings, such as the internal clock, desktop pattern, and other preferences.

14 Copy The menu command used to transfer selected information to the Clipboard without harming the selected information.

9 copying files The process of creating duplicate copies of selected files onto the same or other disk.

19 crash A problem that causes everything on the Macintosh to stop responding to user control.

(1)   **cursor keys**   Four arrow keys used primarily to position the text insertion pointer within editable text.

(14)   **Cut**   The command that deletes selected information and places a copy in the Clipboard.

(11)   **database**   A type of program that contains any type of information divided into individual records (like filing cards).

(12)   **default**   Standard settings provided by a program without any further intervention by the user.

(10)   **desk accessory**   A program, always accessible via the Apple menu, that takes up very little memory and is usually focused on one specific application.

(2)   **Desktop**   The underlying area on the Macintosh screen, which contains icons to disk volumes and the Trash.

(2)   **dialog box**   A screen window that provides information to the user or requests the user to enter information.

(5)   **dimmed menu item**   A menu item appearing in grey that does not respond to selection by the mouse.

       diskette   See *floppy disk.*

(17)   **diskette drive**   A mechanism that reads information from and writes to a floppy disk.

(8) (11)   **document**   An information container created by an application.

(11)   **document window**   The screen area through which you view or edit a document.

(4)   **double-click**   A rapid series of two clicks of the mouse button.

(17)   **double-sided**   One type of a floppy disk, capable of storing approximately 800 kilobytes of information.

(4)   **drag-and-drop**   The process of dragging one icon to another and releasing the mouse button.

(4) dragging Clicking and holding the mouse button down while sliding a selected item across the screen.

(14) draw object A graphic element, such as a circle, that can be manipulated as a single entity, rather than a series of pixels (see also *bitmap*).

(5) Edit menu A pull-down menu found in virtually all Macintosh programs that enables cutting, copying, and pasting of information.

(17) eject The process of removing a floppy disk from the diskette drive.

(1) Enter key A special-purpose key that often acts like the Return key but also may have program-specific behavior.

(1) Escape key A special-purpose key that is often the equivalent of clicking an on-screen Cancel button.

(18) extension A file (belonging in the Extensions folder) that extends the functions of the system software.

(12) field A screen space for entering text information, like a blank in a form.

(8) file An element stored on a disk, usually a program or document.

(5) File menu A pull-down menu in virtually all Macintosh programs that contains commands for file-oriented tasks, such as opening, saving, and printing.

(6) file server A volume that appears on one Mac desktop, although the physical disk may be located in another computer, connected via a network.

(9) Find A Finder command that enables you to specify parameters for locating one or more files on disk volumes.

(9) Find Again A Finder command that continues searching for a match to the same parameters supplied in response to the most recent Find command.

(3)   **Finder**   A Macintosh system software program that enables you to organize, erase, and locate disk files.

(17)   **floppy disk**   A soft magnetic material (similar to cassette tape) housed in a hard plastic shell used for storing computer files.

floppy drive   See *diskette drive.*

(6)   **folder**   A screen representation of a container for one or more files and folders.

(14)   **font**   A collection of letters, numbers, or other characters following the same typographic design.

(18)   **font suitcase**   A file containing one or more font specifications for the screen and/or printer.

(13)   **force quit**   A dialog box that enables you to quit a single program that has a problem without disturbing open documents in other programs. Triggered by pressing Command-Option-Escape.

(19)   **freeze**   A problem whose symptoms include no response to any user action except rolling the screen pointer.

(1)   **Function keys**   A series of special-purpose keys on the Apple Extended Keyboard, rarely used in Macintosh programs.

(8)   **Get Info dialog box**   A Finder-based window that reveals details (exact size, created and modified dates, etc.) about any selected file or folder.

(11)   **graphics program**   Any application that enables the user to create graphical information.

(7)   **grow box**   A window control at the lower right corner of document windows that enables you to drag the window corner to adjust the size of the window.

(19)   **hang**   Same as *freeze.*

(3)   **hard disk**   A mechanical device capable of storing large amounts of computer data, resembling the functionality of a large filing cabinet. Hard disk contents are remembered after the computer is turned off.

⑤ Help menu A pull-down menu on the right side of the menu bar that offers access to a program's help system.

⑤ hierarchical menu A type of pull-down menu that displays submenus to items.

⑰ high-density One type of a floppy disk, capable of storing approximately 1.4 megabytes of information. Denoted by an extra square hole punched in the case and an "HD" marking.

② icon A screen representation of an electronic item (e.g., file, folder, disk, menu command).

⑮ ImageWriter Popular dot-matrix printer for Macintosh computers (no longer in production).

⑱ INIT Jargon name for *extension*.

⑰ initialize The process of preparing a storage medium to accept information for later retrieval.

⑥ kilobyte A measure of information capacity, roughly equivalent to 1,024 typed characters.

⑮ landscape printing The Page Setup specification that lays out printed information so that the paper is wider than tall.

⑮ LaserWriter A popular Apple printer, available in many models and configurations, that uses a low-power laser to produce finely detailed text and graphics on paper.

⑩ launch Start a program.

⑰ locked disk A floppy disk whose locking tab is set, preventing information from being written to the disk.

⑥ megabyte A measure of information capacity, roughly equivalent to 1,024,000 typed characters.

⑥ memory A place for temporarily storing information while working with it (see also *hard disk*). Memory contents disappear when the computer is turned off.

(3) menu bar The screen element stretching across the top, containing pull-down menus used to issue commands to the computer or a program.

(1) modifier keys Special keyboard keys (Shift, Option, Command, Control), which, when pressed with other character keys, modify the behavior of those character keys.

(6) mounting The process of making a volume (any storage device) appear on the Desktop.

(4) mouse A palm-sized device (with one or more buttons) tethered to the computer, which you use to control the location of the screen pointer and to cause action by pressing the button(s).

(4) mouse button The pressable switch on the mouse.

(1) numeric keypad A grouping of keys containing only numbers and arithmetic symbols to simplify entering numbers (also sometimes a separate smaller keyboard device).

(14) Open File dialog A dialog box used to navigate through disks and folders to locate a file for opening within a program.

(1) Option key A special-purpose key capable of producing additional characters beyond the standard alphabet, number, and punctuation symbols.

(8) overlapping windows A window organization that enables some windows to partially obscure other windows, allowing many windows to be present and easily accessible.

(15) Page Setup A File menu command that leads to a dialog box with choices for printed page orientation and other printer-specific settings.

(10) palette A small window usually containing icons for a program's tools or graphics choices.

(14) Paste An Edit menu command that places (when possible) the contents of the Clipboard into the active document window.

(3) pixel A single picture element or dot, the smallest item on the screen.

3   pointer   The icon that moves on the screen in response to the rolling motion of the mouse or trackball.

12 **9**   pop-up menu   A menu style, usually found in dialog boxes or document windows, that enables the user to view, on request, a list of choices.

15   portrait printing   The Page Setup specification that lays out printed information so that the paper is taller than wide.

18   PostScript   A printing technology by Adobe Systems that defines characters by mathematical descriptions of their outlines, rather than by an arrangement of pixels. Preferred over TrueType by professional typesetting service bureaus.

15   Print dialog   The dialog box seen after choosing Print from the File menu. This dialog box gives you the choice of number of copies, page range within a document, and other printer-specific settings.

15   printer driver   A file that contains conversions enabling the computer to speak the language of a given printer.

18   printer font   A file that contains outline specifications for a printer to use in producing characters.

10   program   Any application or desk accessory that turns the computer into a tool for working with information or managing the computer.

5   pull-down menu   Choices available by clicking and holding down on an entry in the menu bar.

13   quit   The process of stopping a program and removing it from memory.

6   RAM   Random Access Memory, the memory area used by programs and documents.

13   restart   The process of turning on the Macintosh again without completely shutting down the machine.

1   Return key   Key that behaves similarly to the carriage return key on a typewriter.

6   **root**   The most basic level of a volume, which you see when opening a disk on the Desktop.

12   **Save**   The File menu command that writes a copy of a previously saved, open document to disk.

12   **Save As**   The File menu command used to give a name to a new document or to save a copy of an existing document.

12   **Save File dialog**   The dialog box used to assign a name to a document and to direct the location where the file is to be saved.

14   **Scrapbook**   A desk accessory that enables the storage and retrieval of frequently used information pieces.

18   **screen font**   A file containing specifications for displaying a font in a particular size on the screen.

7   **scroll bar**   A window control element that shifts the document vertically or horizontally to view other parts of a document.

4   **selecting**   Clicking an item or dragging across text to signify what is to be affected by the next command.

17   **SneakerNet**   An informal way of referring to transferring information between computers via floppy disk.

15   **spooling**   The process of letting the computer perform communication with an external device (e.g., a printer) as a background task, while the user works in other programs or documents.

11   **spreadsheet**   A type of application that replicates on-screen the ledger sheet of columns and rows of numbers.

2   **startup**   The process of powering on a Macintosh and loading system software from a disk.

3   **startup disk**   The volume containing the system software the Macintosh uses to start itself. Appears as the topmost icon in the upper right corner of the Desktop.

16   **Startup Items folder**   A special folder nested inside the System Folder whose contents are started each time the Macintosh starts up.

(15) StyleWriter A popular Apple printer model using ink-jet technology, capable of near-laser quality printouts.

(20) surge protector A device inserted between your computer and the power outlet that prevents sudden high-voltage surges from reaching and possibly damaging the computer.

(6) System folder A special folder containing all files necessary for Macintosh system software to load and operate.

(10) TeachText A simple text-editing program, supplied with Macintosh system software.

(14) text cursor A style of screen pointer used to establish the position of the text insertion pointer.

(11) text editor A program that enables you to type and edit text characters.

(14) text insertion pointer A flashing vertical line between characters that indicates where the next typed character will be inserted.

(8) tiled windows A window organization that places windows side-by-side so that no window overlaps any part of another window.

(7) title bar The window element stretching across the top of the window that displays the window's title and which is used for dragging the entire window around the screen.

(10) toolbar A thin series of graphical screen buttons that usually act as shortcuts to common menu commands.

(4) trackball An alternative device for controlling the screen pointer. Trackballs are built into PowerBook models and are available as options for all Macintoshes.

(9) Trash The icon on the Desktop where files and folders are dragged to be deleted; also where floppy disk icons are dragged to be ejected and file servers to be unmounted.

(18) TrueType A printing and screen display technology by Apple Computer that defines characters by mathematical descriptions of their outlines, rather than by an arrangement of pixels.

14 Undo The Edit menu command that takes back, when possible, the last command that altered a document.

20 virus A dangerous, usually hidden program written by sociopaths that can cause erratic behavior with your Macintosh, including damaging the hard disk. Its effects can be thwarted by virus detection programs.

6 volume A storage device or file server whose icon appears on the Desktop.

15 zone A group of networked Macintosh users set up to be in a network separate from another group.

7 zoom box The clickable window control at the upper right corner of most windows that toggles a window's size between its optimum size (as defined by the program's designers) and the previous size.

Epilog

What To Do When You Don't Know What To Do

My goal with this book was to equip you with basic Macintosh skills so that you could begin using the computer as a productive part of your daily work life. I avoided all the minutiae that Macintosh power users relish. If you should develop a genuine interest in computing as an end unto itself (instead of computing as a means to accomplishing your job), there are plenty of books, magazines, and user groups to satisfy every curiosity.

If you're like most readers, you will soon develop patterns for the way you use the Mac that you won't even think about. You'll tend to start up the same program(s) day after day. You'll cut, copy, and paste the same way day after day, whether choosing the commands in the Edit menu or adopting the command-key equivalents. When using your computer daily, you will develop habits similar to those developed by drivers—like instinctively reaching for the headlight switch in your car as it gets dark. When you get to your destination, you may not even remember exactly when you turned on the lights.

Although knowing basic skills is critical to being productive with the Macintosh, the true measure of proficiency is how well you handle unexpected situations. I have been preparing you for that all along.

Unexpected Situations

The 20th Encounter showed you how to confront any of those hangs, freezes, crashes, bombs, or bugs that get in your way. Do your best to remain calm and follow the suggestions for each problem listed in the 20th Encounter.

Another situation likely will involve figuring out how to perform a procedure you're not familiar with—or uncovering whether the desired action is possible with the software you're using (including the Finder). Master the following sequence, and you will always find what you need:

1. Pull down each menu in search of a familiar command.

2. Try each menu command ending with an ellipsis (. . .) to find clues in dialog boxes.

3. Consult the Help menu.

4. Look for help in the product's manual under every relevent term you can think of.

5. Get help from real people at product support or your corporate help desk.

Fear No More

Despite the apparent complexity of personal computers, especially if you are a newcomer, it is easy to be an intelligent user. No one should expect you to know it all. It's far more important to know where to begin looking for help—somewhere between the menu bar and technical support—than to worry about having all the answers on the tip of your tongue.

If you began this book with fears about using the Macintosh, I sincerely hope that practicing the basic skills in the preceding encounters have shown you how easy Macintosh computing can be. Overcoming fear of the unknown takes just a little practice—most of which you've already had. Now it's time to put your newly acquired skills to work, doing what you do best.

Relax and flourish.

Answers to Exorcises

1st Encounter

1. d

2. a

3. modifier; they modify the behavior of another key pressed at the same time.

2nd Encounter

1. startup; booting
2. icon
3. 3, 2, 4, 5, 1

3rd Encounter

1. Finder
2. desktop; the Desktop
3. pixels
4. Clockwise from upper right corner: e, d, c, b, a

4th Encounter

1. select
2. Pressing the mouse button; rolling the mouse; releasing the mouse button
3. double-click the icon

5th Encounter

1. Clockwise from upper right corner: g, b, a, c, d, e, f
2. Clockwise from upper right corner: f, g, j, h, i, d, c, b, a, e
3. The menu selection leads to the display of a dialog box.
4. g, d, f, h, i, c, b, a, e

6th Encounter

1. 25 working days

2. folder, program, document, document, program, folder, volume, volume, document

3. 20M

4. FileMaker Pro, Finder, Microsoft Excel, PrintMonitor

5. None of the programs are hidden (all icons are active).

7th Encounter

1. Clockwise from upper right corner: c, f, d, e, b, a, and g.

2. a. Allows us to resize the lower right corner of the window; b. scrolls the contents of the window down one line or unit; c. scrolls the contents of the window down one window-full; d. allows us to move the window around the screen.

3. Click the close box; choose Close Window from the File menu; type Command-W.

8th Encounter

1. Select the icon and choose Get Info from the File menu; view window contents in any text mode and see what it says in the Kind column; double-click the icon to see whether a blank document opens in the program or whether the selected document opens.

2. The folder is empty.

3. a. Dragging the file first to the Desktop and then to the destination; b. Change view to any text view, expand all necessary folders, and drag the document to the destination, allowing for autoscrolling the window if necessary.

4. The document will stay in the Hard Disk level, because the destination folder is not highlighted.

9th Encounter

1. a. Duplicate the file and drag the copy to the destination folder;
   b. Option-drag the file to the destination folder.

2. Perform a More Choices Find to locate all document files that are older than a certain date, checking the all at once checkbox. If those documents can be deleted, drag them all to the Trash in one move or, copy them to a floppy disk as an archive of important files and then trash the copies on the hard disk.

3. Search for all files whose modified date is today's date, checking the all at once checkbox. Drag the found files to the other volume.

10th Encounter

1. Both are programs that have their own menu bars, appear in the Applications menu, and modify the About item in the Apple menu.

2. Desk accessories generally occupy much less RAM than applications; they also occupy a single window on the screen and do not have multiple document windows, as applications may provide.

3. a. Click the window of the inactive desk accessory to activate it;
   b. Choose the desk accessory item in the Applications menu; c. Re-choose the desk accessory from the Apple menu.

4. a. Look for the name of the program appended to About in the Apple menu; b. Look for the check mark next to the program's name in the Application menu.

5. Only Information Manager, the active application, is visible on the screen; all others are open, but hidden.

11th Encounter

1. It's up to the program designer. Often, a visual clue is an active Open menu command while another document is already open.

2. The total usually depends on the amount of memory assigned to the program and in your Macintosh.

3. Document windows are resizable and usually sport places for scroll bars. A zoom box is not a prerequisite.

4. Try in the following order: a. typing a few characters to see whether they reach the window; b. look for a New command in the File menu; c. look for a tools palette and select a tool to use with the pointer; d. look for menus that lead to dialog boxes; e. read the manual.

12th Encounter

1. File menu

2. Save assumes that the document already has a name and location in a folder, so it doesn't query you for naming the document; Save As leads to a dialog box requesting a file name and folder location.

3. True

4. Use the Finder to copy the document; using Save As changes the name of the current document to the name of the backup document—the next Save will be to the backup, not the original.

5. You haven't made any changes to the document since it was last saved.

6. The command triggers the Save As command.

7. Each time you reach a point at which you don't want to re-do work because the power went out or the computer hangs.

13th Encounter

1. File menu

2. **Don't Save**: discards all changes and closes the document or program; **Cancel**: takes back the quit command, leaving you at the same spot you were before issuing the command; **Save**: saves the current state of the document before closing the window.

14th Encounter

1. The Scrapbook can contain many pieces of information, but the Clipboard contains only one; the Clipboard is wiped clean when the Mac shuts down, but the Scrapbook stores its contents on the hard disk.

2. Cut and Copy

3. Paste

4. Select the old text and start typing the new.

5. You can't. You need the Clipboard to move information into and out of the Scrapbook.

6. a. Select the paragraph with a click at the beginning and Shift-click at the end; b. Choose Cut from the File menu; c. Position the text insertion pointer at the desired location; d. Choose Paste from the File menu.

15th Encounter

1. The printer driver selected in the Chooser.

2. a. Choose Print from the File menu; b. Tab to the range fields and type 5 and 10 into the fields; c. Click the Print button.

3. Background printing sends information to the printer page by page as the printer is able to accept data, but you can go about doing other

tasks. You can be working in a different program while a long document prints.

16th Encounter

1. Choose Control Panels from the Apple menu to view the folder window containing all control panel files; then double-click the panel of your choice.

2. a. Open the General Controls control panel; b. Click on the hours digits; c. Type the number for one hour ahead of the time displayed there; d. Click the small clock icon to set the internal clock.

3. The computer or a program that's running wants your attention, either because you tried to do something that isn't allowed at that moment or because your input is required to complete a task.

17th Encounter

1. Double-density and high-density diskettes, respectively.

2. A message tells you how much space needs to be emptied to allow the file to be copied.

3. Absolutely. A floppy disk is like any volume.

4. Drag an individual file to the Trash to delete the file from a floppy. To erase a diskette, select the diskette icon and choose Erase Disk from the Special menu.

18th Encounter

1. a. Select the folder; b. Choose Sharing from the File menu; c. Click the `Share this item and its contents` checkbox; d. Close the dialog box; e. Click the Save button.

2. a. Open the Chooser; b. Click the AppleShare icon; c. Double-click the name of your colleague's Mac; d. Click the Guest button and the OK button; e. Double-click the name of the volume; f. Close the Chooser.

3. c, a, b

19th Encounter

1. Extensions are programs that automatically load upon startup and run in the background independent of your actions; control panels, some of which load into memory during startup, give you control over settings that affect your system or external devices.

2. **Extension**: An alert that says you can't open the item; **Control panel**: The control panel window opens; **Font suitcase**: A text listing of font files packaged together in the suitcase; **Font file**: A window showing samples of the font in various sizes; **Desk Accessory**: The desk accessory window

3. The System File also consists of many pieces, some of which we can drag into and out of the file as objects (e.g., sounds).

Index